Türk/Zehe

Acoustic Guitar

From Beginner to Intermediate Level

D1493694

Voggenreiter

Cover:	OZ, Essen (Katrin & Christian Brackmann)
Photos:	Dieter Storck, Bruno Kassel (p. 109)
Editor:	B&O
Translation:	Sylkie Monoff
Setting & Layout:	Notengrafik Werner Eickhoff, D-79100 Freiburg i. Brsg.

© 1999 VOGGENREITER VERLAG
Viktoriastr. 25, D-53173 Bonn
www.voggenreiter.de

English Edition © 2006 VOGGENREITER PUBLISHERS

ISBN: 3-8024-0246-4

TABLE OF CONTENTS

Preface

Why another guitar method for beginners? True - there are plenty guitar books available at every music store. But the authors of this new guitar method are convinced that there is something that has been missing:

That is, a guitar method that keeps the student's mind open for **all musical styles** and doesn't limit them to only one musical direction;

a guitar method that provides the student with music they are **familiar** with, i.e. **pop music**;

a guitar method that slowly and gently introduces the student to **classical** music and offers a carefully selected choice of song examples in this field;

a guitar method that introduces **staff notation** and music theory in a simplified way that is **easy to understand**;

a guitar method that includes a CD which does not only support the student's **practise** but is **fun** to listen to as well;

a guitar method that teaches the beginner a **playing technique** which is useful for any musical style in the future.

Some Words On The Structure Of This Book

This guitar method is divided in three major sections: Section A teaches you the first simple chord fingerings with which you will soon be able to accompany the first songs. In section B you learn the first notes and many old and new melodies. Finally, section C shows you how to combine these two techniques and how to play quite "advanced" pieces on the guitar all by yourself.

There are two ways in which to use this book. If you would like to accompany songs first, you should start with **section A** and then proceed with **section B**. However, if you would prefer to play **melodies first, you should start with section B and then go to section A. But you have to master both sections A and B before you can continue with section C.**

With Or Without A Guitar Teacher

Even if you don't have a guitar teacher, you can learn how to play the guitar with this book. We, the authors, have explained everything in detail. This is especially true for the right- and left-hand postures and the finger movements. So if you study all by yourself, we recommend that you pay careful attention to the descriptions because this book will be your teacher.

This also applies to all other aspects of guitar playing: When do you need to change strings and how do you do that? What should your fingernails look like and how do you take care of them? Where do you buy other equipment? etc. Everything you need to know in this respect can be found in the appendix on page 169.

Some Words About Practicing

Here's a little story: Tim is learning to play guitar. His teacher told him to practice two and a half hours per week. Tim is eager and does exactly what the teacher tells him. On the day before his lesson, he always practices 2 and 1/2 hours. However, after some months he starts to wonder why he doesn't seem to be making any progress. His classmate Tina doesn't practice more than him either; still she can play much better. What is she doing differently? Well, the answer is simple: She doesn't practice 2 and 1/2 hours **once** a week but **five times** 1/2 an hour. OK?

So the first secret lies in the **regular practicing**. The second one is to practice at a **quiet place** all by yourself. Avoid by all means to practice in a room where your brothers and sisters are playing noisily or the TV is running. OK?

It is great if you have a specific workspace, e.g. in your bedroom, with everything at hand that you need for practicing. You don't want to search the whole house for this book before you sit down, do you?

There's another major secret. When you play a piece of music, you will always come across parts that seem difficult for you. That's absolutely normal because every piece consists of parts that are easier and others that are more difficult. When you practice, it doesn't make any sense to start playing the song from the top over and over; you will continously stumble over the first difficult spot. Therefore, it is better to take a close look at this **difficult part** by taking it out of the song and playing it **slowly**. Try to approach the problem step by step like a private detective: Did you read the notes correctly? Are you using the correct fingers? Are you holding the guitar the right way …? Once the problem has been solved, you can "insert" the part back into the song and start from the top. Do you know what I mean?

How long does it take until you will be able to play all the songs in this book the way they sound on the CD? That's a tough question. Of course, this depends on your age and on the hours you spend on practicing. It might take you about 2 to 3 years.

Some Words For the Guitar Teacher

Some aspects of this guitar method are different. We have built the music around the student and not the other way round. This is especially true for section A, the song accompaniment. The use of certain chords is always based on how difficult the fingering is. Therefore, complete cadences will of course be introduced later on.

Music theory is presented in small steps and always in **combination** with the music. We only explain the things that can be put in practice right away.

In this guitar method, every aspect that is **different** from the common approach has been checked regarding the following principle: Is the development of a good guitar technique improved or prevented? For example: Does our "common" sitting position, which can already be found with Sor, get in the way with the classical position? Does the song accompaniment when played with a pick and learned at an early stage prevent the student from acquiring a correct arpeggio playing later on? Or is it harder for the students to learn the C-major cadence later if they started off with the simple chords Em and Cmaj7?

Introduction

The Guitar And Its Equipment

How To Hold The Guitar

The Playing Position Of The Right Arm

Are You Tuned? – How To Tune The Guitar

A Guide Through This Book

The Guitar And Its Equipment

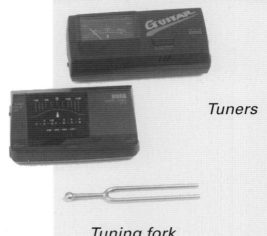

Tuners

Tuning fork

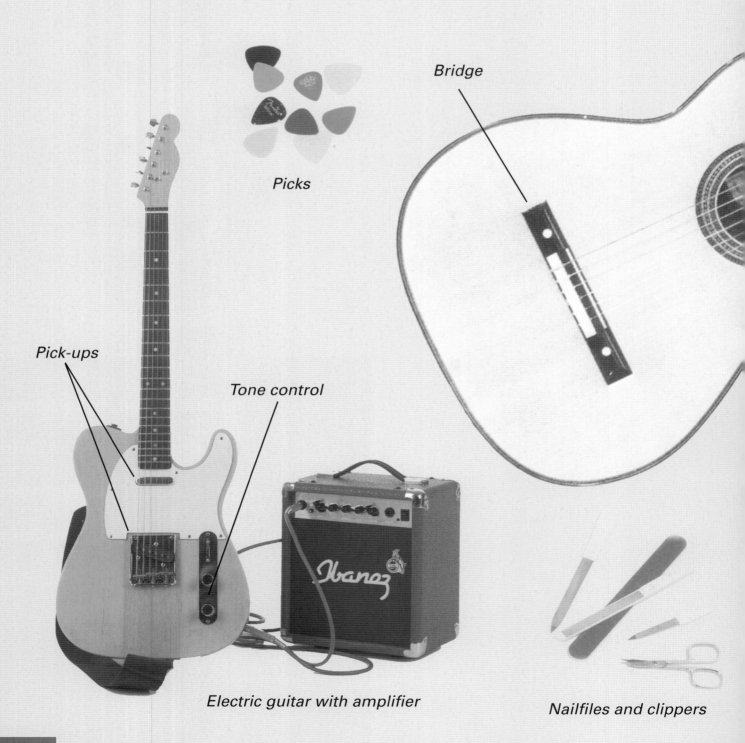

Picks

Bridge

Pick-ups

Tone control

Electric guitar with amplifier

Nailfiles and clippers

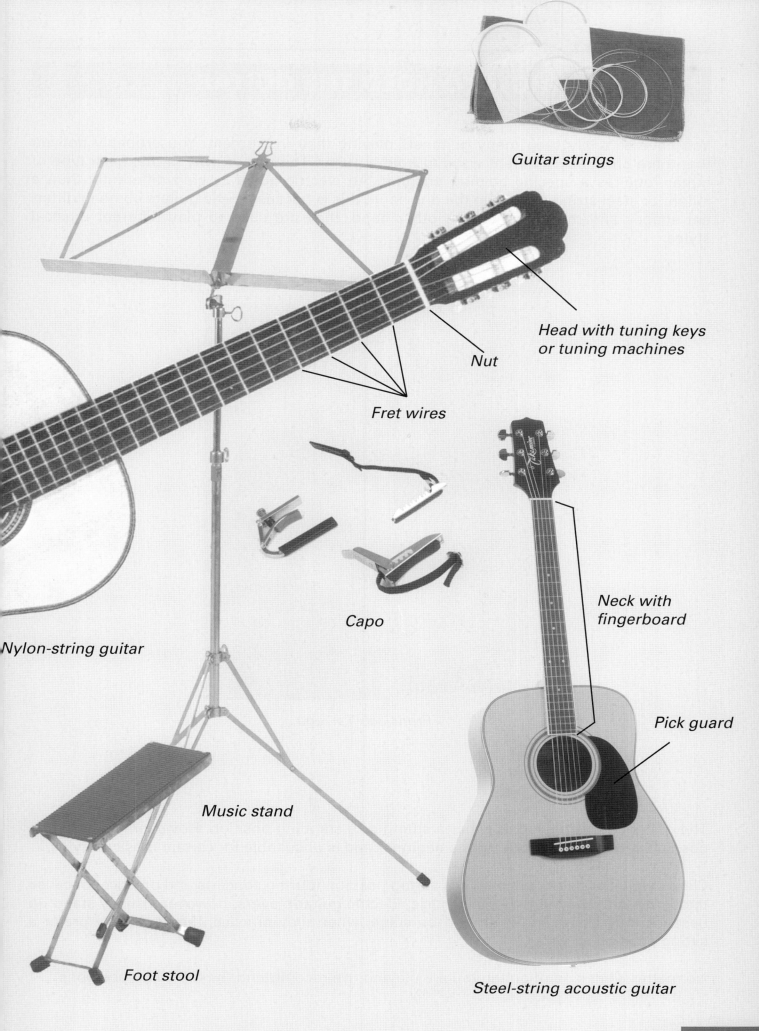

Guitar strings

Head with tuning keys
or tuning machines

Nut

Fret wires

Capo

Nylon-string guitar

Neck with
fingerboard

Pick guard

Music stand

Foot stool

Steel-string acoustic guitar

HOW TO HOLD THE GUITAR

You have certainly seen many guitarists playing their instrument. You probably noticed that there are many different ways to hold a guitar. The reason why is that each type of guitar requires a specific holding position. An electric guitar is held differently than a nylon- or steel-string guitar. On the one hand, this is because these guitars come in different shapes and measures; on the other hand, they are used to play different musical styles.

Francisco Tàrrega

The guitar can be played in either a sitting or a standing position. However, the standing position seems too difficult for the beginner and is unsuitable for certain musical styles.

Classical guitarists always play in a sitting position (during concerts and practice) because that is the **only** way to play their music. Electric guitar-players, however, usually stand up because they like to move around on stage; when they practice, they probably prefer a sitting position as well.

No matter what kind of guitar you are playing, we recommend the following positions.

This Is How You Should Hold The Guitar!

The "Common" Position: Almost Anything Is Possible

First you need a place to sit. Only use chairs that have a level seat but no armrests. The **height** of the chair is very important! Your thighs should be more or less horizontal.

Now the **right** leg is elevated by approximately 10–15 cm, depending on how tall you are. For this, you may use a foot stool or, **in the worst case**, a stack of books. The waist of the guitar should rest vertically on your right thigh.

This is how it should look:

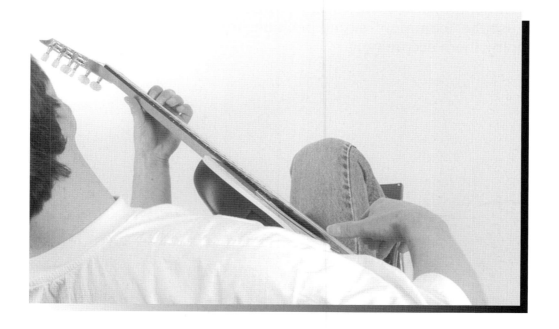

The "Classical" Position: Traditionally accepted

In contrast to the "common" sitting position, the foot stool is used to elevate the **left leg** for the "classical" sitting position.

Guitarists that play classical music choose this sitting position. Most chords are easier to play for the left hand this way. However, for many playing techniques used in pop music it is better to use the "common" sitting position. Try to familiarize yourself with both positions and employ them accordingly.

The Playing Position Of The Right Arm

Let the right elbow rest on the guitar and the right arm hang loose (heavy) towards the floor. The right upper arm is resting on the guitar.

Feel your right hand. Let all your fingers hang effortlessly. Imagine you were holding a small ball. Try to hold it with little effort (loosely), don't push it.

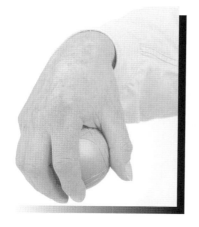

Keep your hand relaxed while moving your forearm upwards so that your right hand can reach the guitar strings.

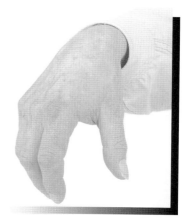

ARE YOU TUNED? – HOW TO TUNE THE GUITAR

The guitar is an instrument that requires constant tuning. The slightest changes of temperature or air moisture can get it easily out of tune. Tuning the guitar without technical equipment is a difficult thing that requires experience. However, you still don't need to practice on a guitar that is out of tune.

There are two simple ways to tune the guitar:

1. On the CD you find **tuning tones**. Each guitar string is plucked five times and then rings for some time. Listen to each tone on the CD for a while. When the note starts to fade, try to match that particular string to the pitch. We start with the sixth string, which is also the thickest one.

2. Use an electronic **tuner**. These little helpers can be purchased quite inexpensively at every music store. They will show you if your strings are tuned correctly or if they're too high or low and need to be adjusted.

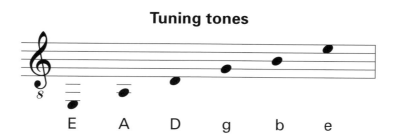

Tuning tones

E   A   D   g   b   e

The small knobs on the guitar head are called **tuning keys**. Think of them as the ears of your instrument. You will find out quickly that the tone gets higher when you increase the string's tension and lower when you reduce it.

A GUIDE THROUGH THIS BOOK

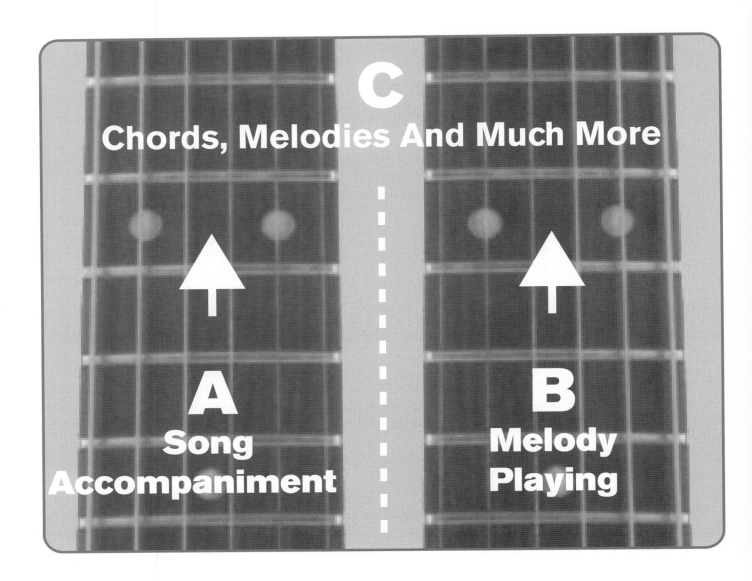

C Chords, Melodies And Much More

A Song Accompaniment

B Melody Playing

Now let's get started ...

A

The Song Accompaniment

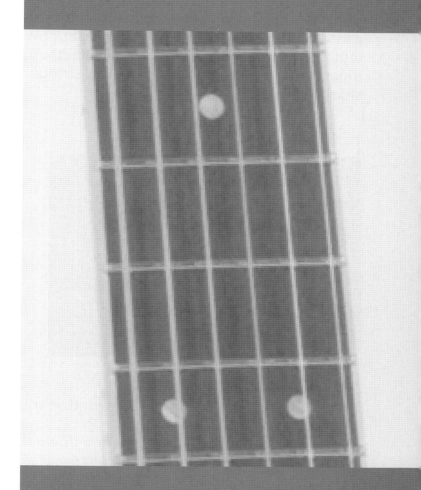

1. THE FIRST STEP IS ... THE EASIEST

We want to start with a song right away! It uses only two **chords**.

What exactly is a **chord**? This is quite simple: Everytime the strings are struck with the right hand, we can hear chords. In fact, even when you don't use your left hand at all, we can still hear a chord. Let's try this right now. Take a soft pick and place it between thumb and first finger of your right hand. Whether a pick is large or small, drop-shaped or triangular, you should always strike the strings with the tip only. **Don't** play with the pick's side!

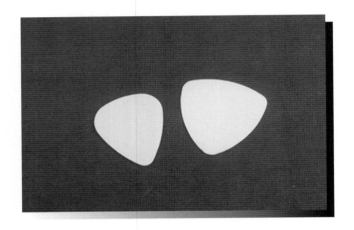

Now all strings are strummed down. Guitarists call this **downstroke**.

In musical notation, the symbol for a downstroke is:

Avoid pressing the pick too much between your thumb and first finger!
Hold it in a way that it can barely glide out of your fingers!

Don't strum the strings too hard!

You can also strike the strings without a pick and use the fingernail of your first finger instead. The thumb always presses **slightly** against the first finger:

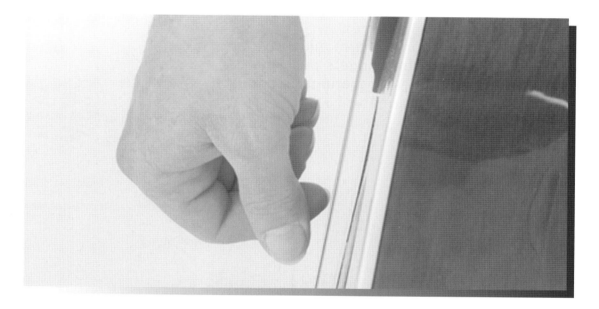

Strumming without a pick sounds better when the fingernail of your first finger isn't trimmed too short!

It's a question of your personal taste whether you choose playing with or without a pick. Try both ways for each new song to see what you like better.

Now listen to the following tune. First you will hear a "count-in", i.e. the drummer of your accompanying band the hits the Hi-Hat eight times. (Count to four twice: 1234, 1234.) Start playing along with the band on the next 1. The chord we are striking without using the left hand can be used for our first song. It helps us to practice the stroke.

By the way: The black dots you can see in this first piece are notes. But don't worry. You won't really have to deal with them in section A of this book. The notes are not meant for you but for your teacher. You can also hear them on the accompanying CD.

Play It!

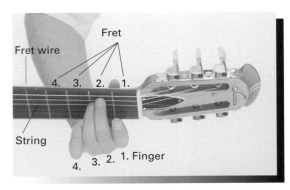

In order to create other chords (harmonies), we need the left hand. The left-hand fingers push the strings on the fingerboard. These **fingerings** create new tones and chords.

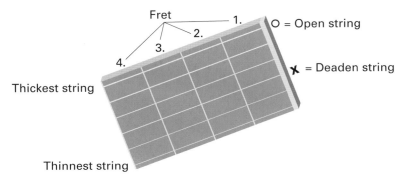

O = Open string

✗ = Deaden string

We only need two chords for our first tune.

In a **chord diagram**, chord 1 looks like this. **Chord diagrams** will be used to illustrate chords. They're easy to understand:

Here are the two chords with their corresponding chord diagrams:

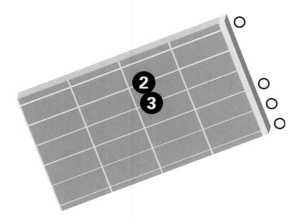

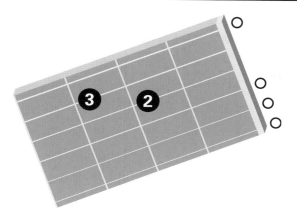

OK, now we're almost ready to start with our first song. Let's first talk about where **exactly** your fingers have to be placed on the fingerboard. When looking at the photos, you probably noticed that the fingers are not placed in the middle of the fret ...

... but **just before** the fret wire.

Wrong!

Right!

The fingernails of the left hand must be as short as possible so that you can push the strings properly!

There is much more to say about the left hand. However, we will get to that later on. Once again, here is the positioning of the left hand and fingers from different views:

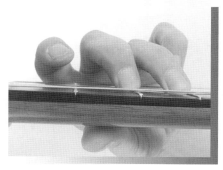

For this song, the whole band plays the count-in which consists of eight beats. (This applies to most of the song count-ins on the CD.) **You** have to start with chord 1. Strum this chord four times. Then strum chord 2 four times, again chord 1 four times etc.

I Play Guitar
1st Version

2. THE NOTE EXPRESS

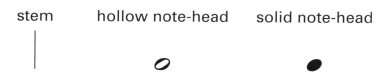

stem   hollow note-head   solid note-head

The way a note looks tells us about the length of its sound. Musicians distinguish different types of notes. Notes with a solid note-head are shorter; notes with a hollow one are longer.

We're now getting to know three **types of notes**:

The quarter note, the half note and the whole note.

In the first song we played, each chord was strummed four times. That means we played four quarter notes:

The half note lasts twice as long as one quarter note:

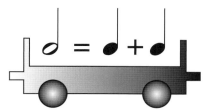

The whole note lasts four times longer:

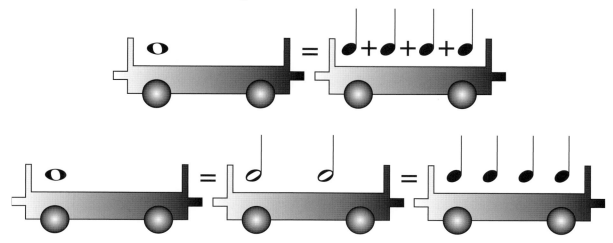

Just like we use letters to form words, we need the different types of notes to form **measures**. These measures are separated by **bars**. In our book you will find a number in a box at the beginning of each line, such as [1] or [5] etc. These indicate the number of the measure you're at. This is very helpful when practicing with other musicians. If a part in the middle of the piece is not working yet and you want to avoid playing the song from the top over and over again, simply say: "Let's try measures [5] to [17] one more time."

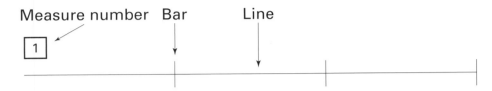

Of course there are many different time signatures; the first one we're learning is called "common time" and designates 4/4 time. One measure lasts as long as four quarter notes:

You can listen to this exercise on track 4 of the CD. On the left channel, a drum plays the quarter notes; on the right channel, you can hear the different types of notes. Try to clap your hands along with the exercise. By the way, the same types of notes can also be found in the following piece.

Clapping Exercise

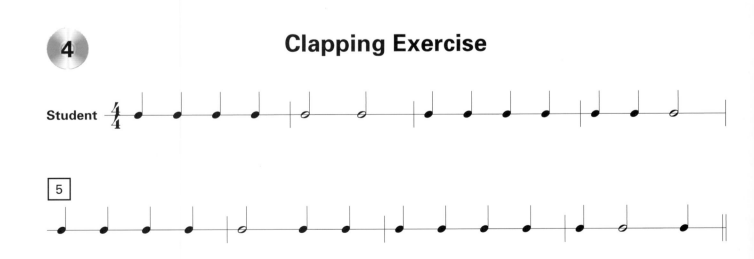

This is a slow piece with feeling. Its melody rises like the sun over your chords. Don't play the chords too loudly. The double bar that you encounter in the next song for the first time divides a piece of music into bigger parts.

Sunrise

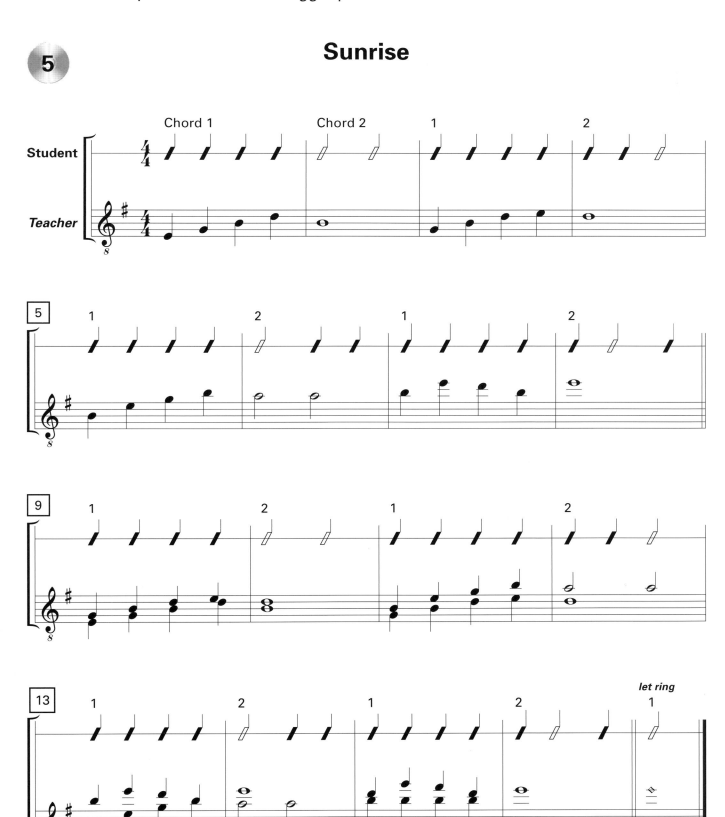

In the next piece, we're going to practice the types of notes with our two chords one more time. You can strum a little harder now and go a little rock. Play the chords loudly this time.

Rock Off

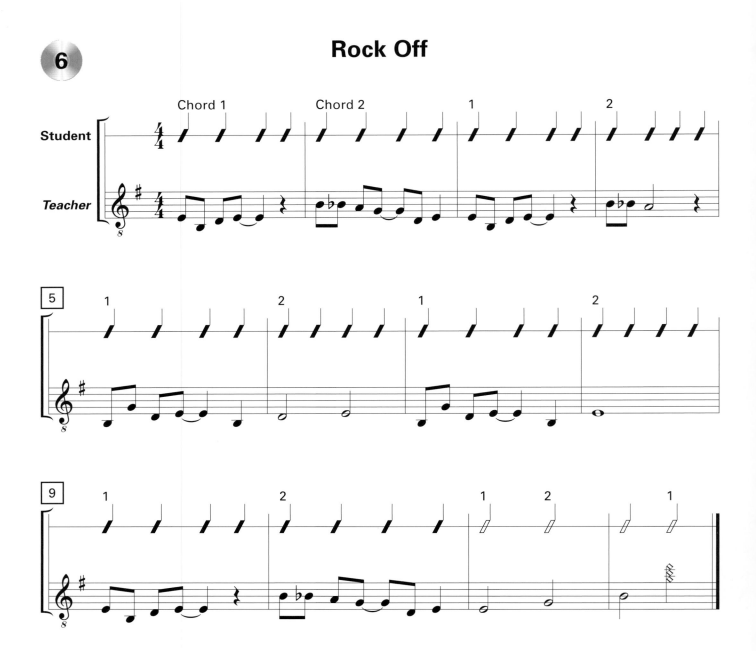

3. WE WANT MORE ...

Chords Have Names

Up to this point, we have only worked with two chords. Of course, there is plenty of others. Our music will become more and more interesting and diverse with every new chord that we learn.

Chords have names such as F-Major, C-minor, A♭maj7, E7♭10 or C13. That sounds quite complicated. But don't be afraid because we will learn it all step by step. I'm going to tell you later how the chords receive their names. For now it's enough for us to remember the names of the chords we're dealing with at this point.

The two chords we've been using so far have a name as well. Chord 1 is called Cmajor7 and chord 2 is called E-minor. And that's what we will call them from now on. Guitarists also refer to these chords by using the short forms **Cmaj7** and **Em**.

Cmaj7

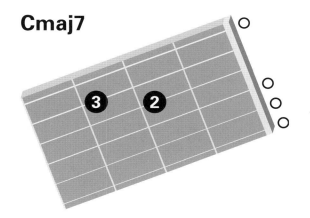

Em

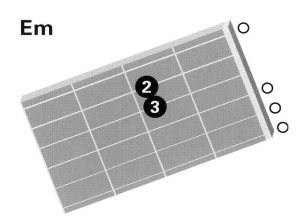

A New Chord: G6

G6

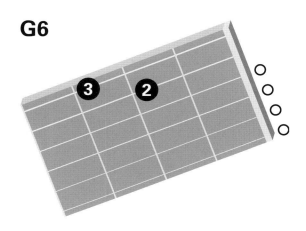

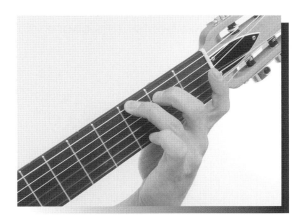

Our next song only needs one chord: G6.

Brother John

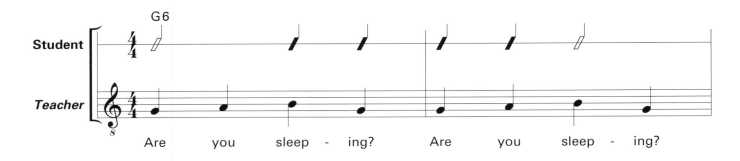

Student

Teacher

G6

Are   you   sleep - ing?   Are   you   sleep - ing?

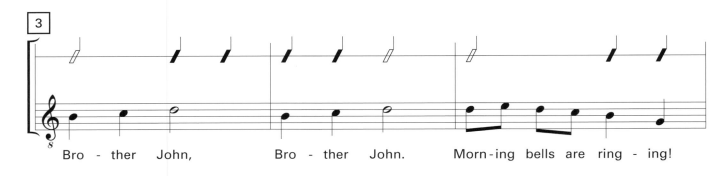

3

Bro - ther   John,   Bro - ther   John.   Morn-ing bells are ring - ing!

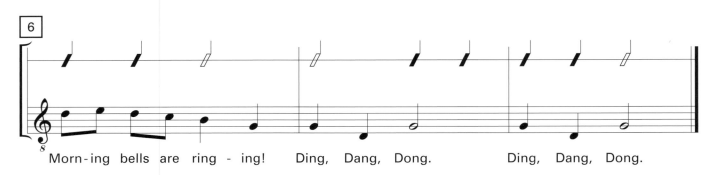

6

Morn-ing bells are ring - ing!   Ding, Dang, Dong.   Ding, Dang, Dong.

Another New Chord: A-minor

The chord symbol for this chord is: **Am**. "**M**" always refers to a minor chord.

Am

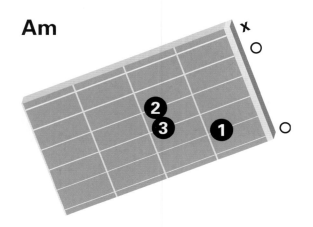

A New Type Of Note: The Eighth Note

The notes we have already encountered are now joined by the eighth note. It lasts only half as long as the quarter note. That means two eighth notes fit into one quarter note.

A New Stroke: The Upstroke

Up to now, we have played all chords using the downstroke, i.e. hitting the strings from the thickest to the thinnest one. However, when playing eighth notes we have to hit the strings twice in the time of a quarter beat; therefore, we use the hand's upward movement for an additional stroke, the so-called **upstroke**.

The sign for the upstroke in music notation is: $\vee$

As the upstroke isn't that easy to perform, we should spend some time practicing it.

In the beginning, your pick will most likely get stuck in the strings. This can be avoided by a slight twist of your arm.
Imagine you were sitting at the breakfast table and you would like to fix yourself a peanut-butter sandwich. In order to save time, you will move the knife in two directions, back and forth. You will notice that you're holding the knife differently depending which way you're moving your hand.

Do the same thing with your pick. It's very important that you slightly twist your whole forearm!

By the way, it is OK to only hit two or three of the thin strings when playing the upstroke. This way the chords also sound brighter and lighter.

We will practice this technique in the next piece by replacing the **third** quarter note of the measure by two eighth notes.

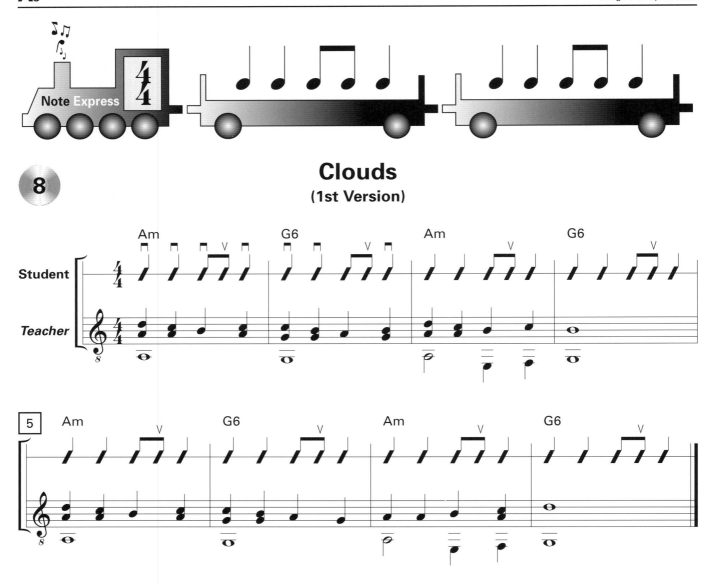

Clouds
(1st Version)

Use the two new chords **A-minor** and **G6** to accompany the next song. In each measure, the **second** quarter (the second beat) is replaced by two eighth notes now.

Everybody knows the melody of this song. It's a so-called shanty, a song that sailors used to sing during their hard work on the old sailboats. In fact, there is a good reason why they did that: The rhythm of the music helped these men to handle all the tough jobs they had to do on board, such as the tackling of the sails and the heaving of the anchor.
Let's sail off to sea …

What Shall We Do With The Drunken Sailor

What shall we do with the

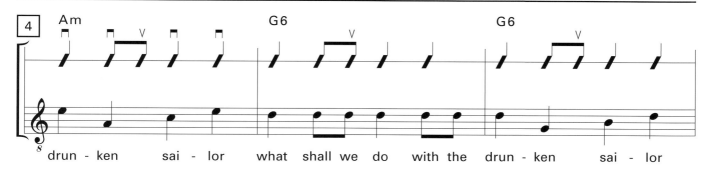

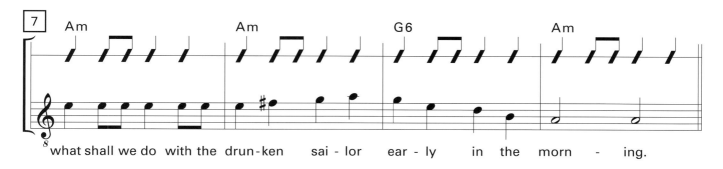

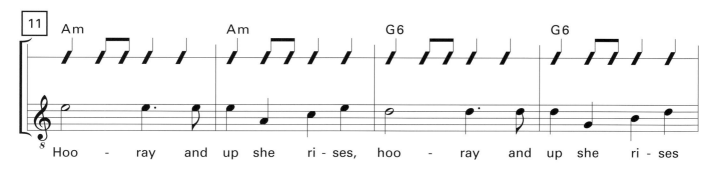

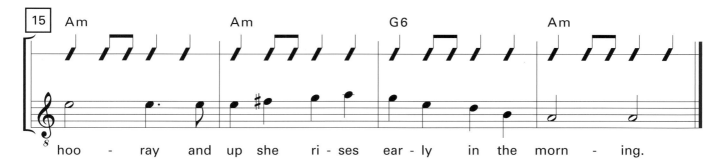

2. Take him and shake him and try to awake him …
3. Give him a dose of salt and water …
4. Give him a dash with a bosom's rubber …
5. Put him in a long boat till he's sober …
6. Pull out the plug and wet him all over …
7. Heave him by the leg in a running bowline …
8. That's what to do with a drunken sailor …

In the last song of this chapter, we are using all chords and note types that we have learned so far.

Heartbreak

4. VISITING FOREIGN COUNTRIES AND PEOPLE / NEW SONGS

In this chapter we're making a musical journey through different countries and continents. We will play known and unknown songs from North and South America, from Spain, Greece, Russia, France and Germany; and we will also learn some new chords and strokes.

Before we can take off, however, we need to put two new chords in our backpack: **C** and **G7**. Chords whose name consists only of a **capital letter** are **always Major-chords**.

The C-Major Chord

Let's first play Cmaj7, the chord we already know:

Cmaj7

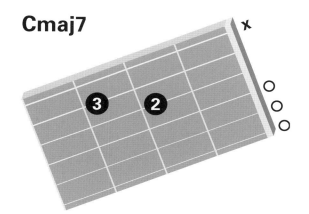

Then place your first finger on the first fret of the 2. string:

C

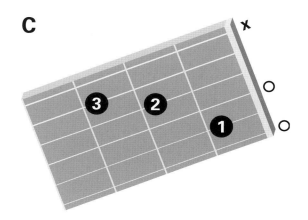

The low E-string is not played for these chords!

Make sure to "square" the **1st finger** and push the string with the tip so that the neighboring **1st string won't be touched**!
Otherwise, it cannot sound properly.

right

wrong

The G7-Chord

First place your fingers on the fingerboard for the G6-chord, which we already know. Then add the first finger by placing it on the first fret of the 1st string.

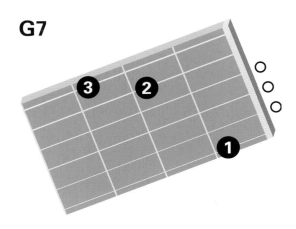

 Make sure to put the **2nd finger** on the string so that it **doesn't touch the 4th string**! Otherwise, this cannot sound properly either.

right

wrong

The change from C to G7 and back is usually not that easy because three left-hand fingers have to be **moved simultaneously**!

In the next song, however, this change is still fairly easy because we're playing the open chord on the fourth beat of each measure. We know this chord already; it consists of open strings only (see page 20, CD-track 02). So you'll have enough time to prepare the fingers for the next chord "in the air".

Repeat Signs

The following piece uses two symbols you haven't seen yet. These are **repeat signs**.

Repeat signs include two double bars and colons. When the colon is written **before** the bold bar, you have to jump back in the song. Now look for the measure where the colon appears **after** the double bar; this is where you start repeating. That means the two repeat signs embrace the music that has to be repeated. Everything inside this bracket has to be played another time. When writing down songs, this can save you a lot of time and paper. Why writing down a melody twice if only the lyrics change but the notes stay the same?

The Journey

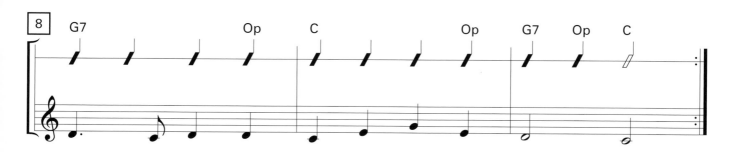

Now we can start our journey with a gospel from North America. Gospels are the church songs of the Afro-American people. The singing also involves dancing and clapping ...

By the way, various famous Afro-American musicians started their career in a gospel choir, such as Stevie Wonder, Whitney Houston, or Janet and Michael Jackson.

Our gospel song is called "He's Got The Whole World In His Hands". It describes how God is holding all people in his hands.

He's Got The Whole World In His Hands

Melody: Trad.

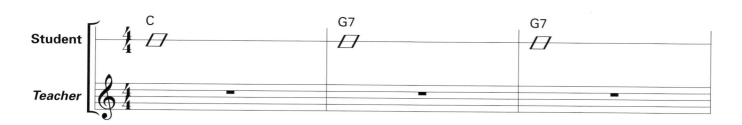

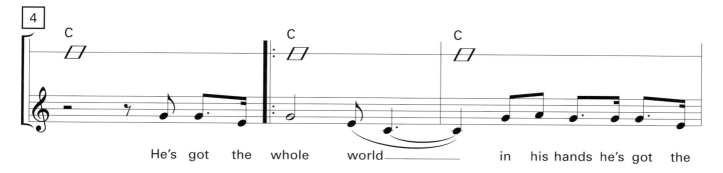

He's got the whole world_____ in his hands he's got the

whole world_____ in his hands he's got the whole world_____

_____ in his hands he's got the whole world in_____ his hands. He's got the

2. He's got the tiny little baby in his hands …
3. He's got you and me brother in his hands …
4. He's got the son and his father in his hands …
5. He's got the mother and her daughter in his hands …
6. He's got everybody here in his hands …
7. He's got the sun and the moon in his hands …
8. He's got the whole world in his hands …

From North American, we jump over to the other side of the globe. This little melody is from Russia.

Childrens Song

And once again we move to America. Somewhere in the south around 1860 Thomas C. Dule was sentenced to death for the murder of Laura Foster ... and in song Thomas C. Dule became Tom Dooley.

Tom Dooley

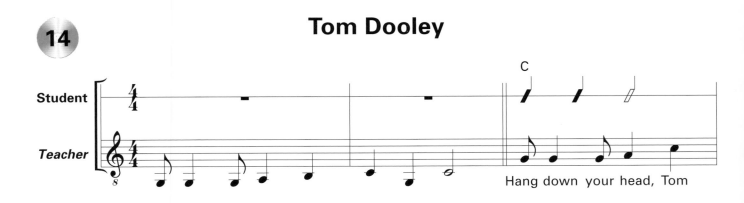

Hang down your head, Tom

This time come tomorrow
reckon where I'll be
in some lonesome valley
hanging from a white oak tree ...
Hang down your head ...

Our journey continues to South America. Nobody knows exactly when it was composed, but it certainly tells a tale of dancing and flirting ...

La Jesucita

Melody: Trad.

The following little melody comes from the far north, from Greenland, the home of the Inuits …

Atte Katte Nuwa

Melody: Trad.

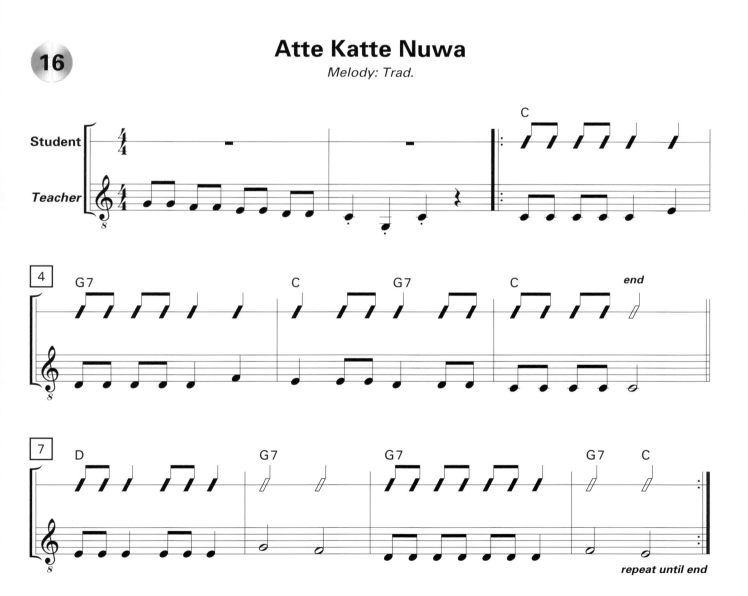

The next jolly melody comes from Alsace. It's a leaping dance tune and it has a new time: 3/4 . Up to this point, we have only played songs in common time (4/4). What is different about 3/4? Well, it's quite simple: 3/4 time has one quarter note less than 4/4, i.e. only three quarter notes per measure. When the first one of these three notes is emphasized, we create a typical waltz feel. This dance-like waltz effect comes out even stronger when you strum the lower strings for the first chord stroke and the higher ones for the following two.

First And Second Ending

In this song, a new kind of repeat sign occurs for the first time. It is necessary when you have to repeat a longer melody passage that has a different ending than before. For this, we use so-called **"first and second endings"**. The respective measures are marked by brackets which are numbered 1. and 2. That means, on the first time through, you have to play the music shown below the 1st bracket. When you reach the repeat sign, go back to the beginning. On the second time through, skip the first ending, and continue with the second ending instead.

German Folksong
Melody: Trad.

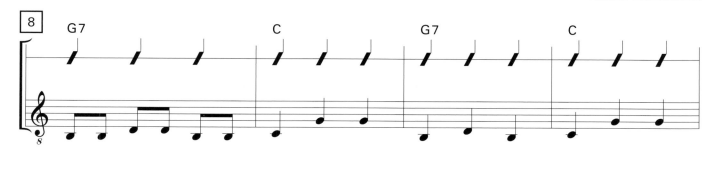

Our journey ends in Spain, the native country of the classical guitar.

For this song, we need to learn the new chord **E7**. Place your fingers in a way that the fourth string can ring clearly.

E7

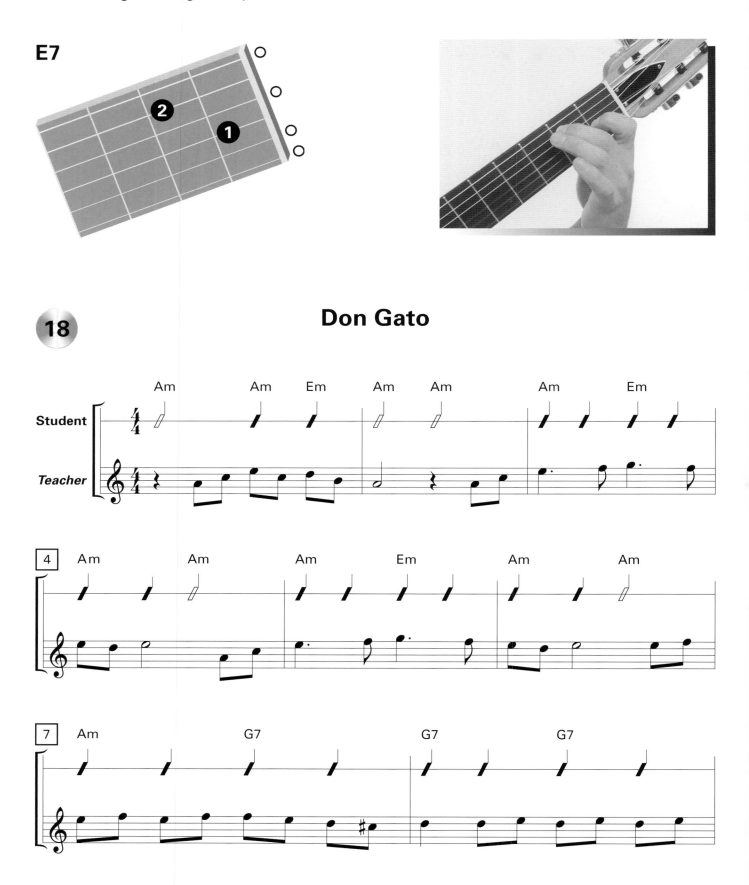

Don Gato

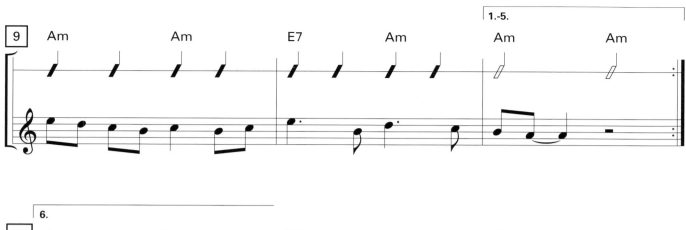

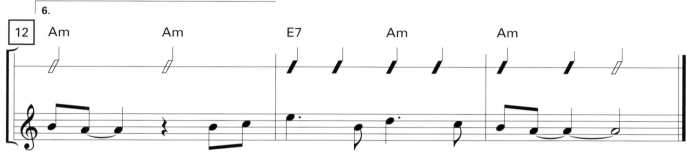

5. YOUR FIRST POP SONGS

Finally, here we go: In this chapter, we're turning to the first pop and rock songs. And on the CD you will of course be accompanied now by a small band including more guitars, a bass, keyboards and drums.

The strumming pattern for the first piece "Short Ride" consists of two quarter and four eighth note strokes per measure. It is maintained throughout the entire song. (By the way: This pattern can be found in many pop songs with an acoustic guitar accompaniment.)

For "Short Ride" we need the two new chords **D7** and **G**.

D7

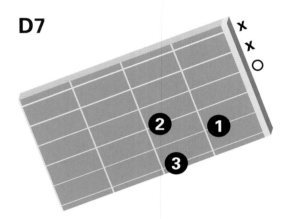

G

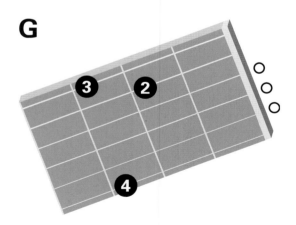

Short Ride

19

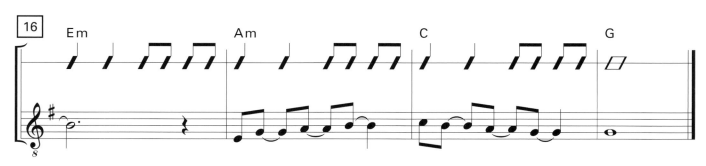

"Funny Tunny" is based on the same rhythmic pattern as "Short Ride;" however, the flow of the music is interrupted several times and seems to still. This is a stylistic device which is often used in rock and pop music to create diversity. Musicians usually call this a "break".

As there aren't any new chords in "Funny Tunny", you can focus completely on the breaks. Also, please pay attention to the final measures 19 and 20: Against our expectations, the final chord Am in measure 19 doesn't start on the **one**, but on the **two**! It will help you immensely if you tap your foot or nod your head on the **one** to fill the quarter rest.

Because of this special notation in the final measures, we have a quarter rest, a dotted half note and a tie reaching into the last measure. More details about the quarter rest can be found on page 77. The dotted note is explained on page 69 and the tie on page 79. (We know that this tune is slightly anticipating the material we'll learn later on – but we really wanted to use this nice song ending for this piece!)

Funny Tunny

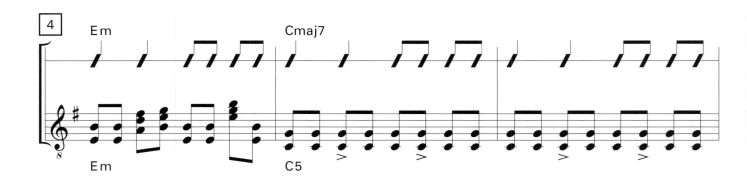

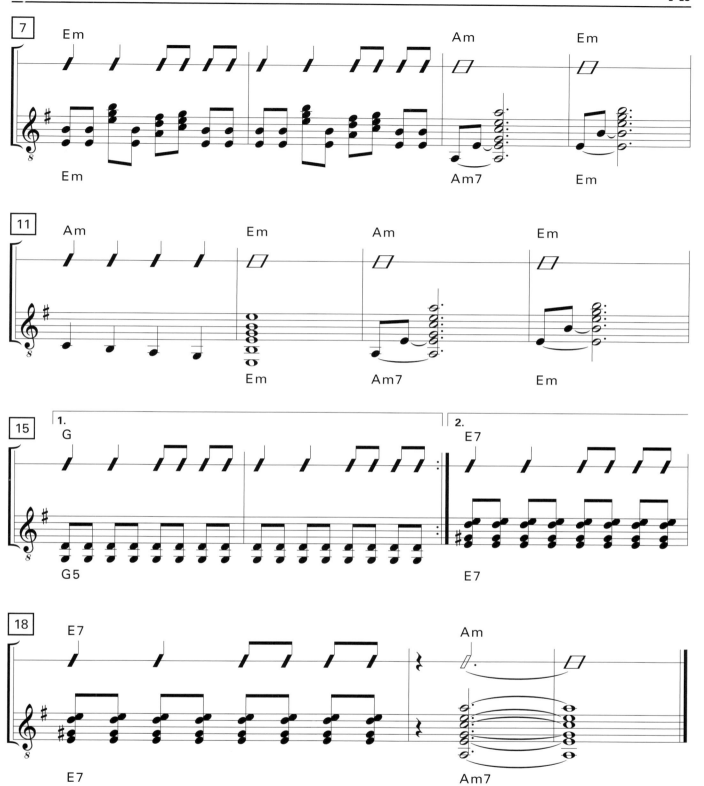

The next song is a ballad, a slow lovesong. We have written this song especially for you.

The song is played with the chords that you already know well: G, C, Em, Am and D7. We have only added one more chord, **A7**, which shouldn't be a problem for you either.

A7

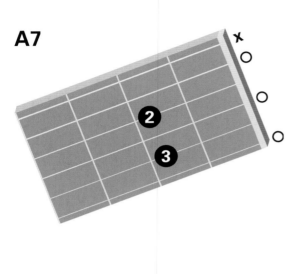

You Are Gone

(1st Version)

2. Come to me, back to me, I know, that you will see,
   there will be harmony, forever

For the following song "There Were Times" we need two new chords: **Gmaj7** and **A**.

The chord **Gmaj7** is very similar to G7; only one "tiny" note is different. However, the sound color is changed immensely. All you have to do is move the first finger a fret up on the first string – what a difference!

G7

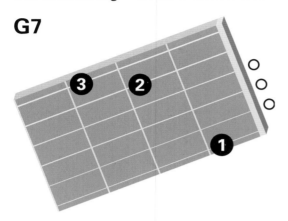

Gmaj7

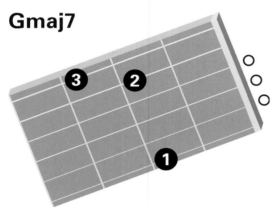

Now we still need the **A-Major chord**. In the previous song, you already learned the A7 chord. Now it's getting a little more difficult. The third finger has to be placed on the second fret as well.

A

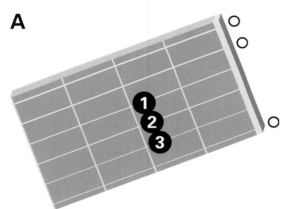

Place the first and second finger on the second fret of the neighboring strings. Although it might seem difficult to find enough space for all three fingers, try to push the strings close to the fret wire. You will need a little patience until this chord will sound clean.

There Were Times

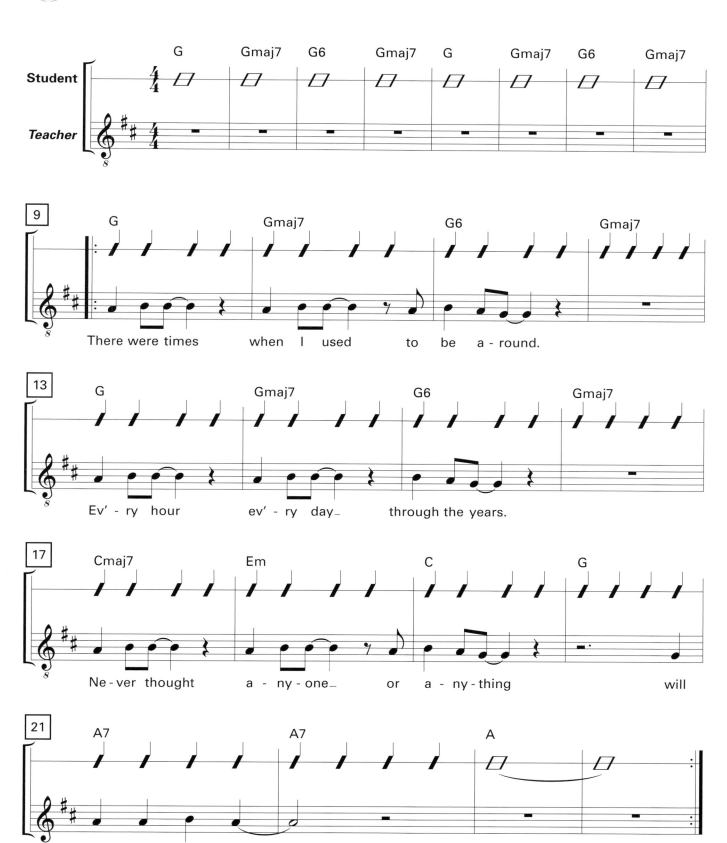

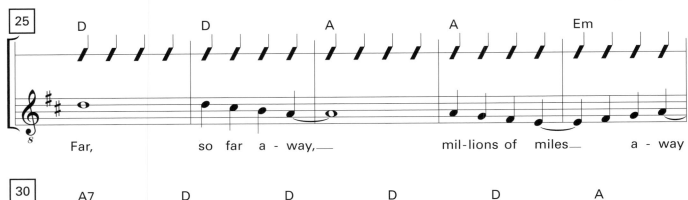

Far, so far a - way,— mil-lions of miles— a - way

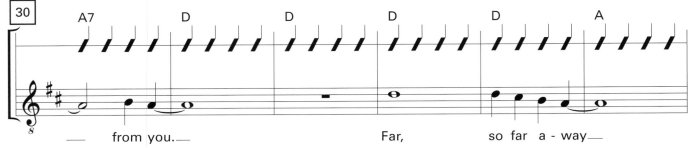

— from you.— Far, so far a - way—

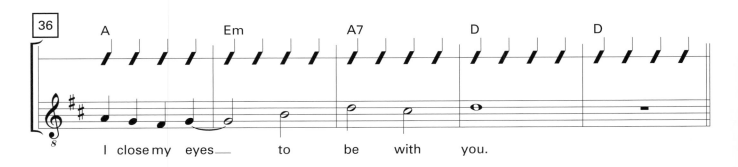

I close my eyes— to be with you.

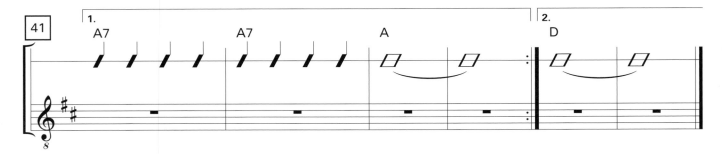

2. Time will come, when I'll use to be around.
   Ev'ry hour, ev'ry day through the years.
   Won't believe, anyone or anything
   will take me away from you.

   Far, so far away …

B

Melody Playing

1. THE FIRST NOTES – THE FIRST PIECE

Notes On The 4. String (D-String)

A melody is a sequence of single tones. To put it simple, a melody can as well be sung because it never has two tones at the same time. In most types of music the melody is in the foreground and is accompanied by chords.

The guitar can play chords as well as melodies. Therefore, you should learn to master both playing techniques to expand your musical options.

Music Notation?! – So What?

Melodies can be written on paper by means of notes. This music notation can be read by all musicians, no matter what instrument they're playing.

You might think that we're talking about a "secret code" that will be hard to decipher. But it's actually not that big of a deal. In fact, notes are immensely useful for musicians and in the end there aren't that many anyway. We're going to learn them step by step.

Notes are placed on, above or below a **staff** consisting of **five lines**. These are numbered upward like this:

At the beginning of each staff you find an odd-looking, twined symbol, the **clef**. There are several different clefs. However, guitarists use only one, the so-called **treble clef or G-clef**. Attached to it, you can see a small "8". This clef circles the second line of the staff, on which the note G is written. This is where the G-clef got its name.

We write our **notes** in this **staff**:

This means the notes show us how **high** or **low** a tone sounds!

But we would also like to know how **long** or **short** a tone is. This can be indicated by the notes as well.

If you have worked through section A of this book, you are already familiar with the different note types. However, if you have started with section B, you should have a look at pages 23–24.

In order to avoid rushing, we will begin playing a single tone with the strongest and most reliable right-hand finger: **the thumb**.

When playing a melody, you can either sit in the common or the classical position (see Introduction page 12-14). Please check these pages again to make sure your sitting position is correct. And now let's begin.

Preparatory exercise for the right hand:

Lean your third, second and first fingers against the third string. The string should be loosely caught between fingertip and fingernail.
The fingers are slightly curled; the third finger is stretched almost completely.

Pull the thumb slightly upward so that it is held above the fifth or sixth string.

Let the thumb drop forward from this resting position with a sudden and swift movement. It is supposed to touch the fourth string as briefly as possible, ...

... then it quickly passes by the resting first finger on the left side ...

... and immediately returns to its starting position (without interrupting the flow of the movement).

Wait until the tone has faded completely. Then repeat the movement.

 The thumb has to strike the string quickly and in a determined and sweeping movement. Don't let it go too deep below the strings because it might get stuck. Then the tones will sound muffled and noisy and the movement will be slowed.

It's better to miss the string every once in a while at first than to pick it too cautiously or slowly.

The tone you have just played is called D. In the staff, the head of this note is placed below the first line.

d

In this song, you play this D-note sixteen times as a quarter note. As the exercise is in common time, the first of the four notes per measure must always be louder than the following three. Count to "4" four times while playing. That way you will know when the louder tone is due.

Rocky
(1st Version)

We are not yet using any other pitch (new note) in this song. At first, three different types of notes (tone lengths) occur, i.e. the quarter, half and whole note.

Before playing along with the CD, you should practice the song by yourself until you can hold the different note lengths correctly and your tempo is steady. Count aloud while practicing and tap the beat of the quarter notes with your foot.

Rocky
(2nd Version)

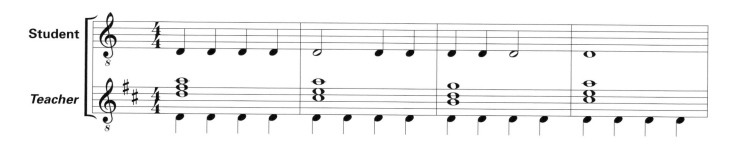

How Do You Position Your Left Hand Correctly?

 If you have worked through section A of this book, you will already be familiar with the left-hand fingering. You should still pay attention to the following tips.

Let the left arm hang down loosely. Take some time to feel the weight of the arm. Now slowly lift the arm and bring it to this position:

The thumb is important:

It is placed on the back of the neck directly across from the 1. fret,

not like this:

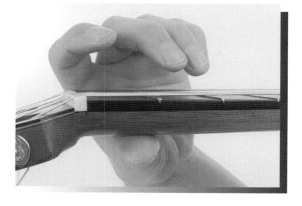

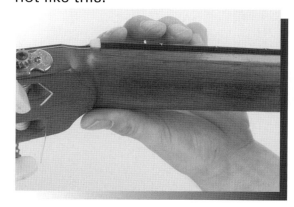

Now push (not too hard) the D-string on the 2nd fret with your 2nd finger. This should look as follows:

 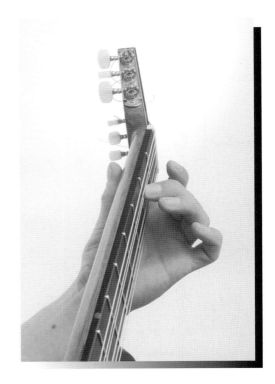

It **should not** look like this:

 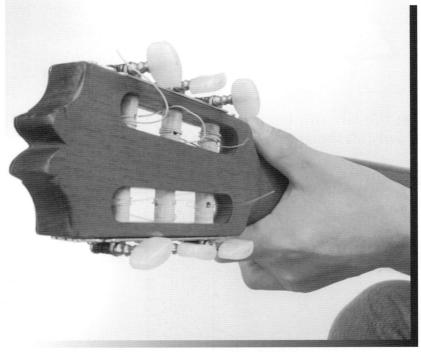

The thumb is too high …   *… the wrist is too high …*

... the 2nd finger is too flat ...   *... the 2nd finger is at the wrong fret.*

Should your fingernails be scratching on the fingerboard although your finger positioning is correct, they are too long.
Trim them short to avoid this! (More about the fingernails can be found in the Appendix).

Now we know how to position the hand and fingers correctly. Let's practice the fingering now.

Tapping Exercise

Slowly count to eight: 12345678, 12345678 and so on ...
At "1", you "tap" your 2nd finger on the D-string. Leave the finger there and lift it off quickly at "5".

Repeat this with the 3rd finger on the third fret. Of course, everything shown above for the 2nd finger applies here as well.

Tones D, E and F

The tone you've just played with your 2nd finger is called E. In the staff, it is written on the first line. The tone you've played with your 3rd finger is called F. Its note head is written in the space between the 1st and 2nd line.

d   e   f

d

e

f

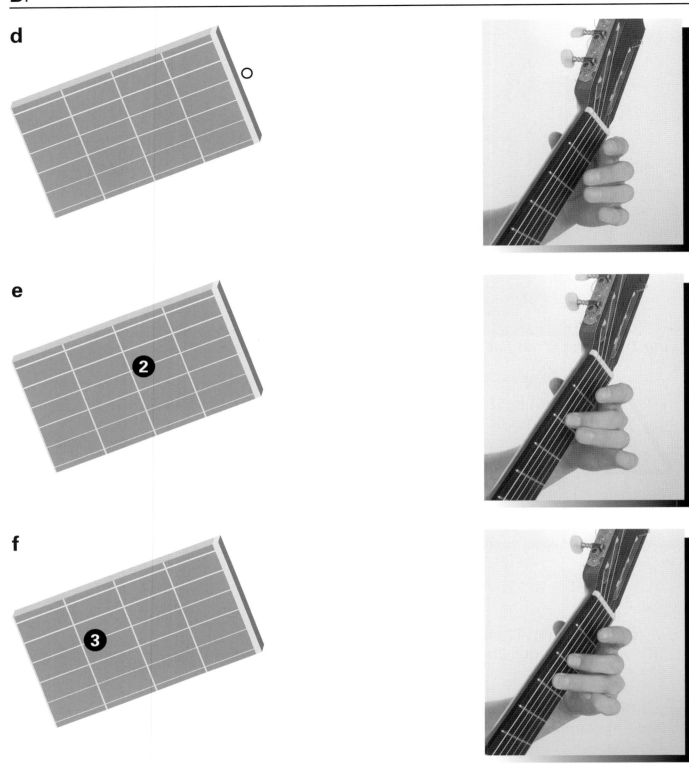

You have probably noticed that there is another fret in between tone D and E on our fingerboard (the first fret); between E and F, however, there isn't. Musicians call a short distance between tones (like between E and F) **half step** and the bigger one (between D and E) **whole step**.

With these new notes we're able to play the next song. It's a lullaby. But be sure not to fall asleep while practicing. Wait 'til you're done with this tune.

Lullaby
(1st Version)

25

The next piece is dedicated to the Hungarian composer Bela Bartok. Not only did he compose complicated orchestra and piano music, but he wrote many little musicpieces for children as well. By the help of these, he wanted children to enjoy learning the piano. That was our intention, too, when we composed the following piece for you future guitarists.

Bela Bartok

Belas Dream

26

2. NATIVE DANCE

Notes On The 3rd String (G-String)

When you strike the third string, you can hear the note G. Place your second finger on the second fret of this string and you'll hear the note A.

g

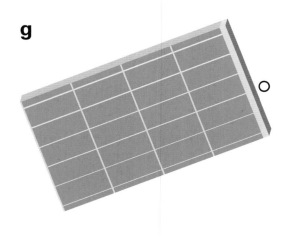

a

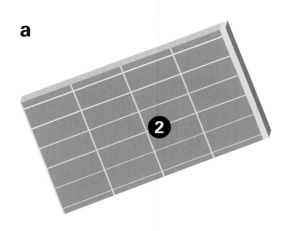

This brief exercise is in common time (4/4) and consists of quarter notes only. Each measure contains the note G three times and A once. Try to learn by heart on which beat A occurs in every measure; then you'll be able to play this piece by memory before long. Make sure to play the first tone of each measure slightly louder than the following ones.

27

Changes

Student

Try to imagine for the next song you were quietly sneaking up on someone. One leg has the tone G, the other the tone A. But watch out: You don't switch from one leg to the other every time!

28

Sneaking

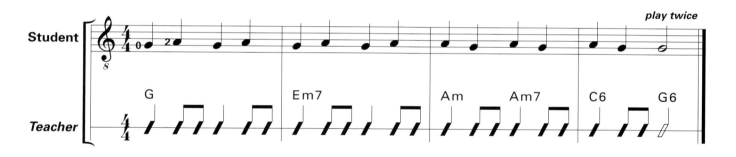

play twice

Student

Teacher

G   Em7   Am   Am7   C6   G6

The hatchet is buried now; let's start to dance. If you like, you can drum on your guitar as well. Lay the guitar across your thighs with its strings down. You can then drum on the guitar bottom with the tips of your third finger and thumb. The wrist is resting on the wood.

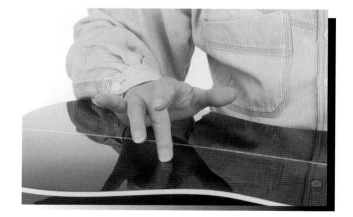

Native Dance
(1st Version)

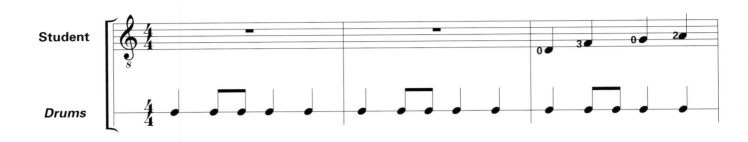

Take A Rest ...

In the next piece you will come across a new sign. It looks like a small beam hanging from the fourth note line.

This is a **whole rest**. It tells you to be silent during the entire measure.

Be silent for **four** beats! (Count to four!) This won't be a problem in the first and second measures of our next piece: We'll simply wait for our cue.

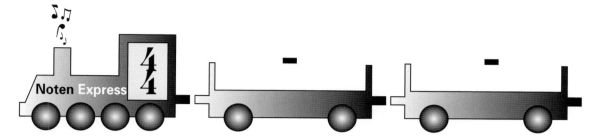

Things look different for the first time in measure 6. Here you have to make sure that you stop the tone that is still ringing from measure 5. Guitarists say that they **mute** a string. To do so, briefly place the right thumb on the ringing string.

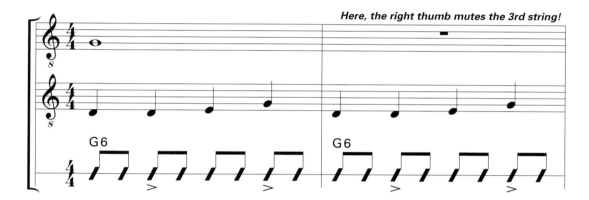

We will learn about other types of rests later on.

Dotted Notes

Here you can see half notes with a dot behind them. A **dotted half note** receives three beats.

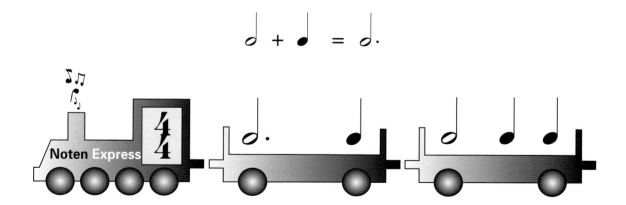

The second student's part sounds better when strummed close to the bridge. The tones will sound brighter and clearer this way.

dark sound

bright sound

After we made it through various adventures in the country, this chapter ends in the Wild West saloon of "Somewhere City".

Me And My Horse

3. A GENTLEMAN NAMED BEETHOVEN

Notes On The 2nd String (B-String)

When you strike the second string without placing your left hand on the frets (open string), you hear the note **B**. The next note on the first fret is **C**; these two are a half step apart. On the third fret, a whole step above C, is **D**.

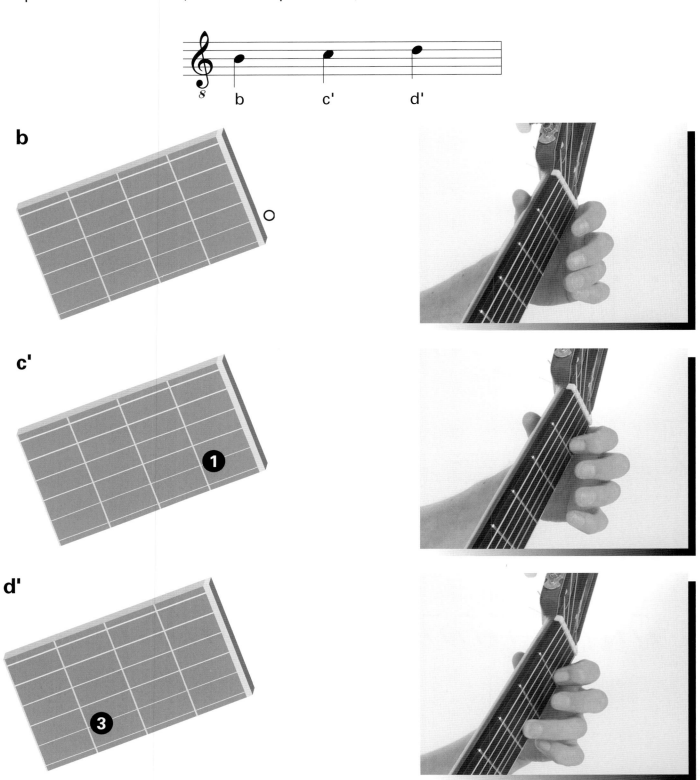

Setting Up And Resting Of The Fingers

In the next song, our left hand will learn something new: The **setting up** and **resting of** the fingers, which is very useful.

The **setting up** works as follows: When a note is followed by a lower one on the same string, we place our fingers on the string for **both notes at the same time**. That means the finger has already been anchored on the fingerboard before the string is struck for the second note – we have **set** the finger **up**. This will make your playing smoother!

In music notation, the setting up is indicated by a horizontal line above the respective notes.

Resting means the contrary: When a note is followed by a higher one on the same string, **we let the finger rest** on the fret of the first note, i.e. the finger is kept on the fingerboard. A dotted line shows you how long you have to rest the finger.

We will apply this technique for the first time in "By The Riverside". But the symbols for setting up and resting will occur in the later pieces as well. So watch out!

Imagine you were on a summer vacation. You're sitting somewhere by the ocean, the sun is setting and the wind is blowing a few small clouds across the endless horizon.

If we wrote the symbols for setting up and resting in the staff each time this technique has to be applied, we would quickly create a vast amount of figures, lines and dots; these would make it only harder to read the notation. Therefore, it is our goal that you will be able to recognize where to use this technique even when it's not explicitly shown in the staff.

By The Riverside

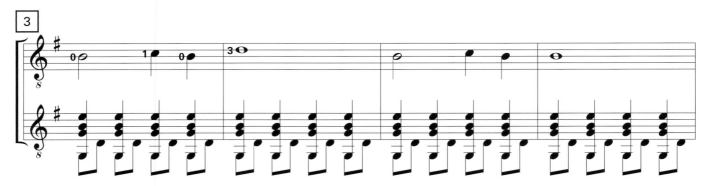

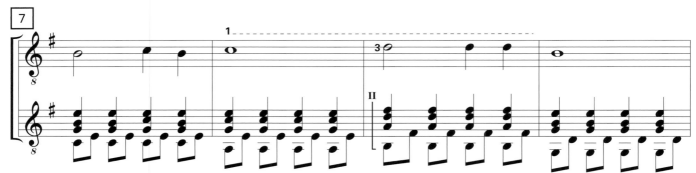

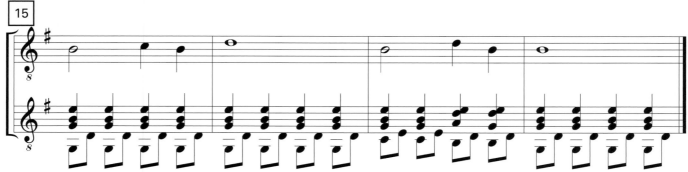

With the help of the new notes B, C and D, we can add another part to the Native Dance you already know from page 68.

Native Dance
(2nd Version)

To play the following piece imagine that you were sitting on board of a glider. You're floating through the air silently and your view …

Clouds
(2nd Version)

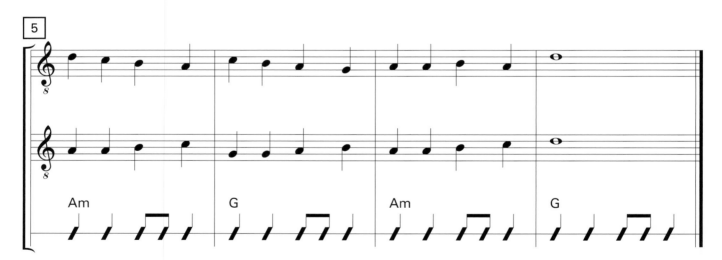

In the next exercise we will play the new notes and also a new type of note: the **eighth note**. This has half the length of a quarter note and looks very similar. There are two ways to write it. If the eighth note occurs alone, it has a flag on its stem. When several eighth notes occur together, the **flags** are replaced by a **beam** connecting the stems.

Exercise

At first, practice each measure individually by repeating it in a "loop". Count while playing. The numbers below the notes tell you how to count.

Student

1 2 3 4 and   1 2 3 4 and   1 2 3 4 and   1 2 3 4

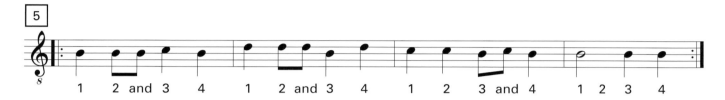

5

1   2 and 3   4   1   2 and 3   4   1   2   3 and 4   1   2   3   4

9

1   2 and 3 and 4   1   2 and 3   4   1   2 and 3 and 4   1 and 2   3   4

Quarter Rest

We have already learned about the whole rest earlier in this book. The whole rest lasts four beats or counts. In general, each type of note has a corresponding type of rest. The **quarter rest** is used in the next piece; it tells you that no tone is to be played for the duration of one beat (quarter note).

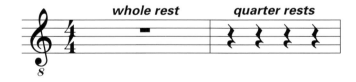

whole rest   *quarter rests*

Noten Express

Summer Dance

When we talked about the whole rests, we learned how to mute a ringing note with the right thumb. This is what we're going to do for the quarter rests in the next piece as well, i.e. for the first time on the third beat in measure 5.

You can play "Summer Dance" slowly and emphasize every note; it will then sound like an old folk dance. If you can already play a little faster, emphasize only the first note of each measure. This way, the music will sound more elegant and lively.

The Tie:
Make One Out Of Two

The next piece presents us with something new: **The tie**. It connects two notes of the same pitch and turns them into one. For example, when you tie two quarter notes …

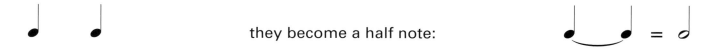

When you tie a half note with a quarter note …

they become a dotted half note:

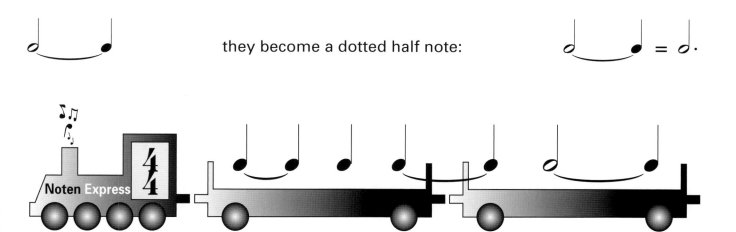

Both can be found in the next little piece.

Jamaica

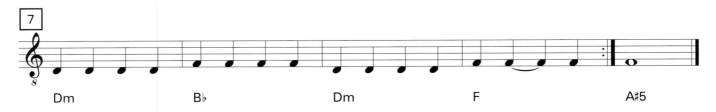

The next piece is our old friend: "I Play Guitar". In section A, chapter 1 we learned how to play the accompaniment. Now we will learn the melody. There are ties in this song as well, this time in combination with eighth notes. Here is a preparatory exercise with counting help:

Exercise

I Play Guitar
(2nd Version)

The following example prepares you for the song "Without Words" on the next page. We're familiar with these types of notes; however, they were not yet used in this sequence. In order to be able to learn the song effortlessly, we suggest you first practice this preparatory exercise intensely.

Exercise

For the next song, we need all the tones we have learned to play on the D-, G- and B-string up to this point.

The melody of "Without Words" has a characteristic that is typical for pop songs and could somewhat be found in the last song already: Certain tones are moved forward by an eighth note and played on the off-beat. In "Without Words" this mostly happens to the last note of a repeated little melody part, the so-called "phrase":

The last note would normally be expected to occur on the one of the following measure; however, it is moved forward to the off-beat on the four-and! This way, melody phrases receive a lighter feel which vanishes immediately when you stop playing on the off-beat. Try it out by playing "Without Words" like this:

It sounds much better with the notes on the off-beat, doesn't it?

Without Words

For the end of Chapter 3, we have arranged a melody from Beethoven's most famous work – the ninth symphony – in a way that you will be able now to play it together with a couple of friends or with your teacher.

Ludwig van Beethoven

B₃

Ode To Joy (An die Freude)

4. WITH THE PINKIE

Notes On The 1st String (E-String)

When you strike the first and thinnest string, you can hear the note E. When you place your first finger on the first fret, you can hear the note F, which is a half step higher. Another whole step up, i.e. two frets to the right, is G.

This is the first time you're using your **pinkie**, the **4th finger** for guitarists.

From now on you will use your 4th finger for a while to play this new note G on the 3rd fret of the E-string. You might be wondering why you can't use the 3rd finger instead just like you do for the D on the B-string. Well, alright … You could certainly do that, too. However, we would like to train the weakest finger, which is the fourth one, and will therefore use it for the G.

e'

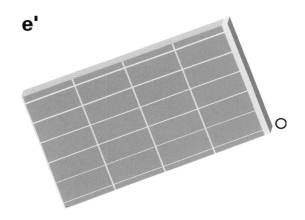

f'

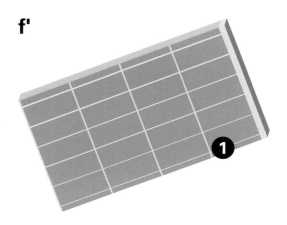

g'

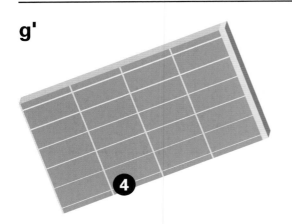
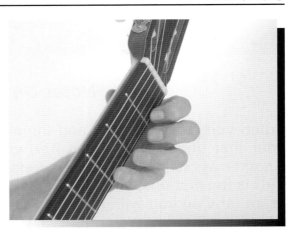

Half Rest

The half rest has the length of two beats and looks like a little beam lying on the line. It can be notated faster than two quarter rests. Everytime it occurs, you have to be silent for two counts.

The following piece is dedicated to Eric Satie. He was a French composer who often wrote very strange pieces but also funny ones. Some sound similar to our tune. (You will find a piece by Satie farther back in the book.)

Mr. Eric

39

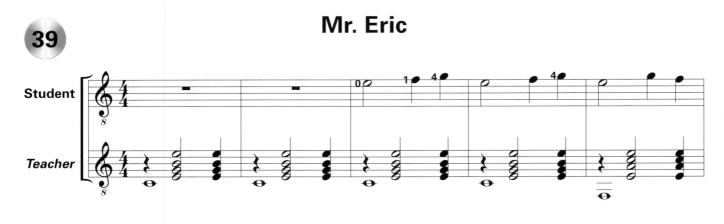

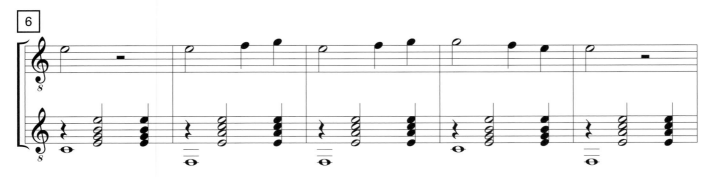

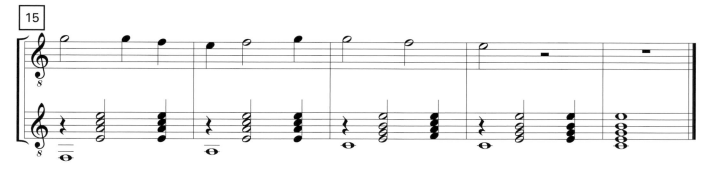

In the next piece we will encounter a new type of rest, the **eighth rest**. It has the same duration as an eighth note, of course.

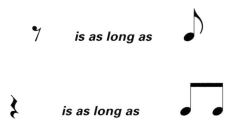

In our next song, "Friends at the sea", the eighth rest appears several times. For this reason, there is a preparatory exercise first. It will help you to learn the piece much faster and better.

Exercise

Perhaps you know the funny stories of the three friends; then you should know big Waldemar as well. One day, after the three friends have gone to a county fair, they decide to take a boat-trip on the near-by lake. This is what the song is about.

Friends At The Sea

You already know "You are gone" from the accompaniment section of this book. We're now taking a closer look at the melody. Enjoy!

You Are Gone
(2nd Version)

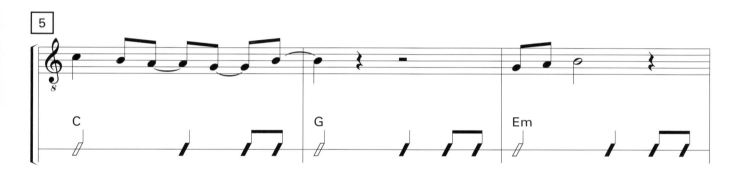

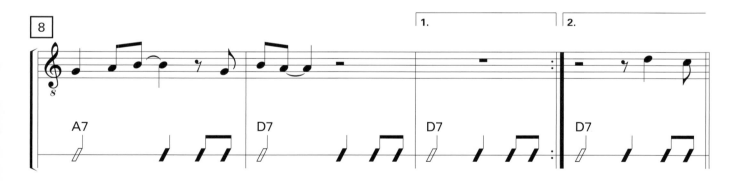

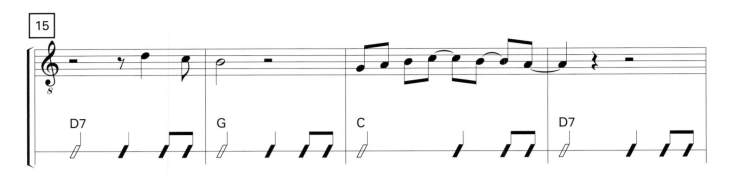

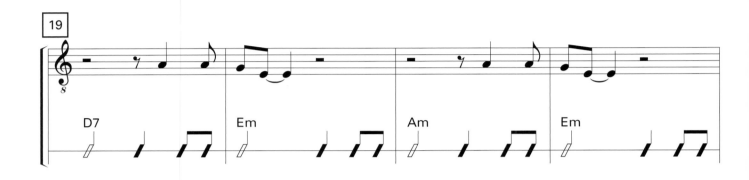

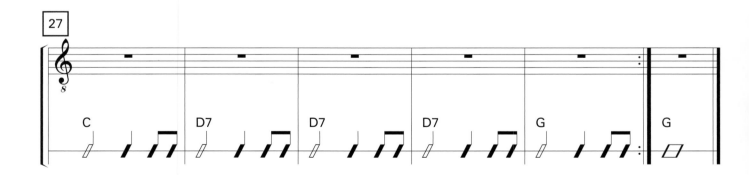

5. MIGHTY LOW

Notes On The 6th String (E-String)

The sixth and thickest string plays the lowest tone of the guitar, the low E. As the tone of the open string is the same as the one of the first string, the notes F and G can be found on the first and third fret as well.

E   F   G

E

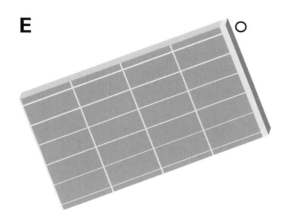

F

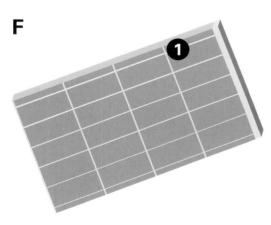

G

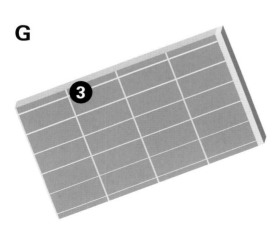

It is usually harder to read the note than to play it. Here's a little help for your memory.

The lowest tone of the guitar is called E. Its note head is written under the third ledger line below the staff. If you imagine the three ledger lines to be the horizontal beams of the capital E and connect them by a vertical line, you will receive the capital E. The note head of note E is written below this letter.

Try to learn the names of these three notes and where they are notated in the staff. It will spare you a lot of time if you don't need to figure out the low notes.

After you have already played the notes of the fourth and first strings, you know by now that F and G are the next higher tones above E. One step up above E you find F on the third ledger line; and another step up, below the second ledger line, there is G.

Our first song that uses these new notes is called "El Toro". The title reminds us of Spain because that is where "El Toro" can be found. Again, let's do a little exercise first.

Exercise

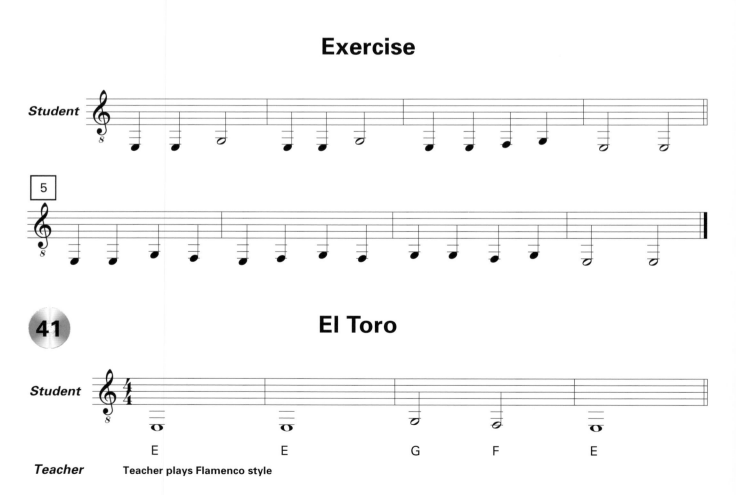

Teacher   Teacher plays Flamenco style

Once again, we would like to practice the new notes with you. This time, however, with a little rock tune. Here, the singers (students #2 and #3) sing the same tones that you are playing on the sixth string of your guitar (student #1). But wait a minute! These tones aren't **exactly** identical; the singers sing tones that have the same note names but they sound a lot higher. We call the distance between two notes of the same name "**octave**".

Student #2 sings the tones an octave above you; student #3 is even two octaves higher than you.

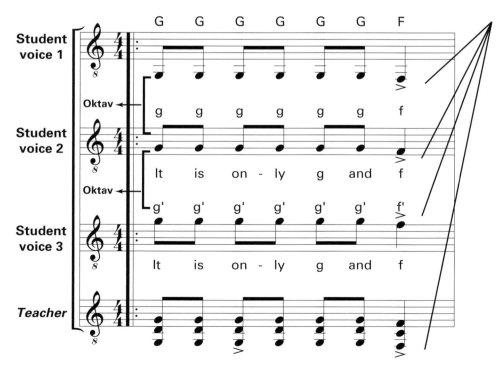

Notes that have an accent mark (>) must be played louder.

Come On

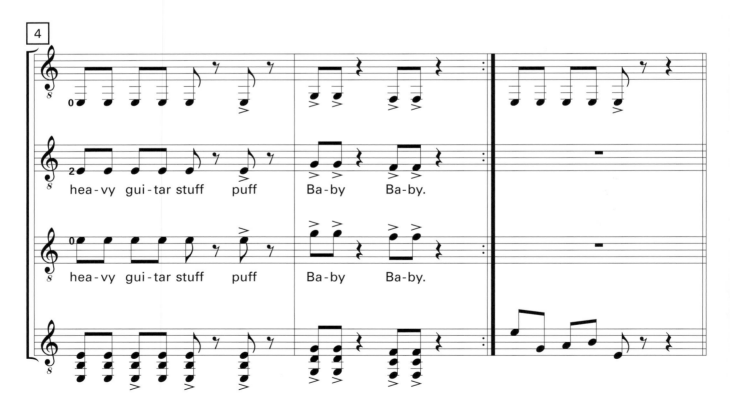

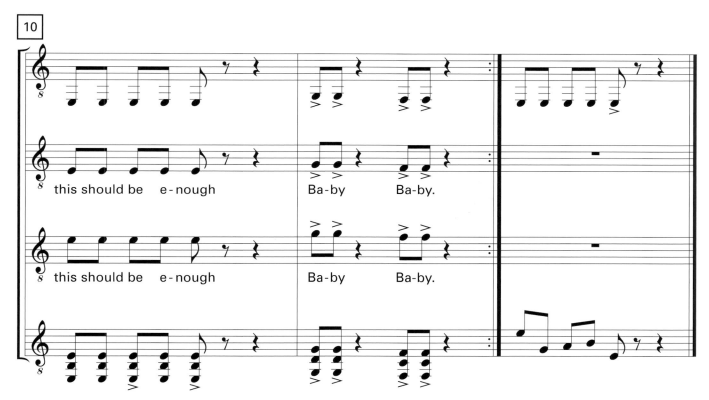

6. ONE IS STILL MISSING ...

Notes On The 5th String (A-String)

Finally, the notes we haven't yet talked about are the ones played on the fifth string. The open string is A; on the second fret, a whole step above, is B. Right next to this, a half step up on the third fret, is C.

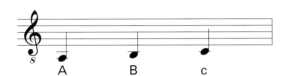

A

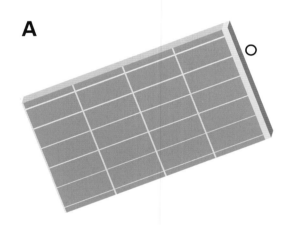 

B

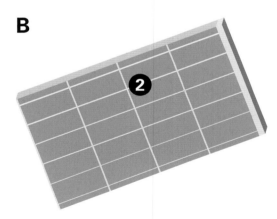 

C

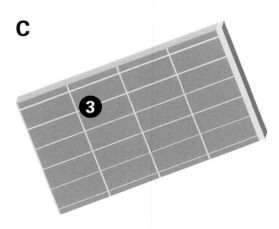 

We will come across a new musical style in the next song, which presents us with all the notes of the A-string for the first time. When you're done practicing, allow yourself to play along with the accompaniment on the CD. You will then realize that this is actually a funk tune.

Funk The A

Chords for the teacher's part in "Funk The A"

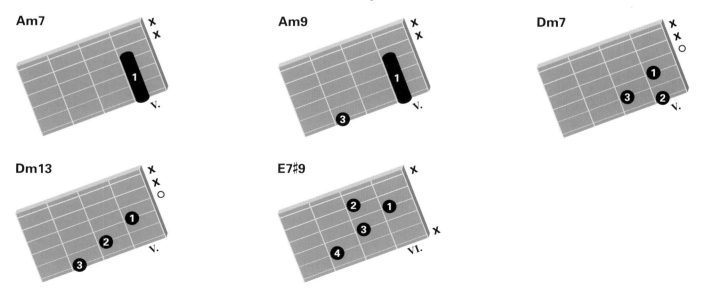

With the next song, we're entering an entirely different musical world. Everything is dark and a bit spooky; the small melody scraps are played on the low strings …
Only twice, a spot of light seems to brighten the dark: In measures 9/10 and 13/14, the melody moves upward to the B-string, but not for too long.

Try to keep these images in mind when playing "Darkness". That way the tones you're playing will come to life.

Darkness

Fingering exercises don't need to be boring. The next song will prove this. It also reviews all the notes you have learned so far. After you have practiced it for a while, you should play it along with the CD or together with your teacher. It really "rocks", believe me! This "final exam" is fun!

Please make sure to keep the fingers on the fingerboard as long as you can when playing upwards; and when playing downwards, remember to place all the fingers needed on one and the same string simultaneously.

Up And Down

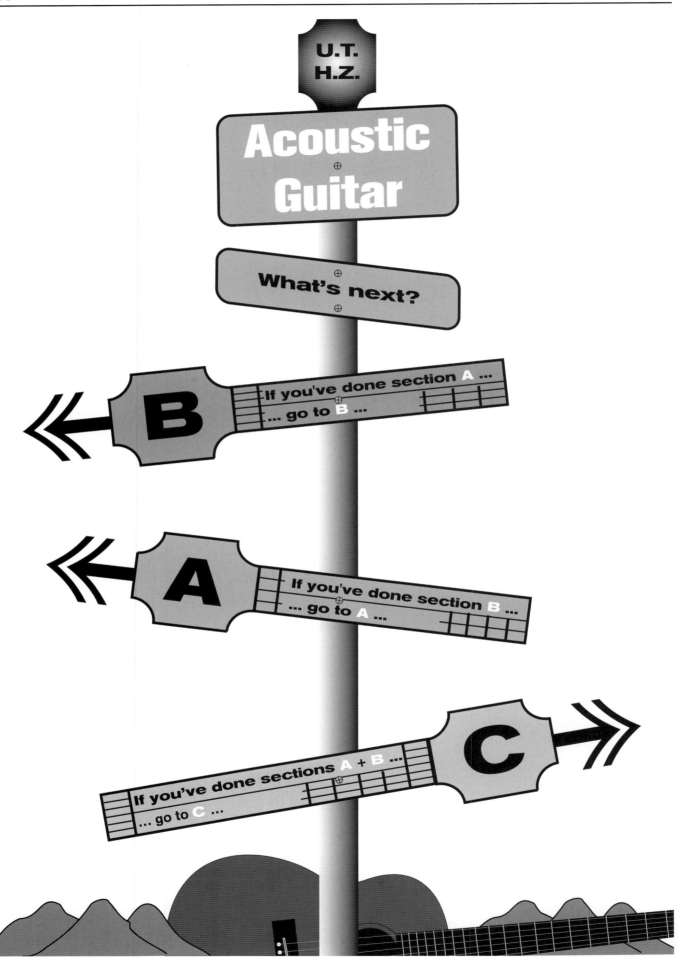

C

Chords, Melodies And Much More

1. ARPEGGIO

So far, we've played all chords in section A with a pick. However, you can also pick the strings with your fingers and play so-called "fingerstyle". Fingerstyle is used when the single tones of a chord are to be played individually and not all at once. That means the chords are **broken apart** or **arpeggiated**.

When we arpeggiate, we use four right-hand fingers: thumb, first, second, and third finger. (The pinkie is not used.) All over the world, guitarists use the following letters to indicate these four fingers:

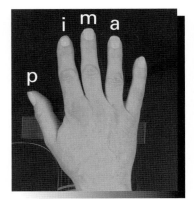

p = pulgar, i = index, m = medio und a = anular.

Before we turn to the first piece that uses this new technique, let's try a short preparatory exercise to help us get familiar with the correct hand position. Take a look at the photos below:

 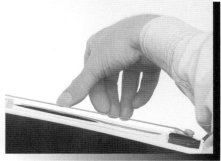 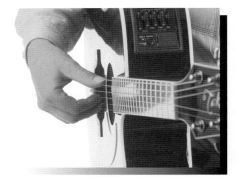

As you can see, all fingers are slightly curled. Imagine holding a small ball in your hand really loosely so that you nearly drop it. Whenever you start to doubt if your hand position is correct, **remember the ball**!

The photos also show you which finger has to pick which string: The thumb is resting on the low E-string while the first, second and third fingers are held below the G-, B- and high E-string.

Note: Don't put your fingers too deep in between the strings!

Now the hand is ready for the stroke. Take a close look at the following six photos before you start with the exercise. The left hand doesn't have to do anything because we're only picking open strings.

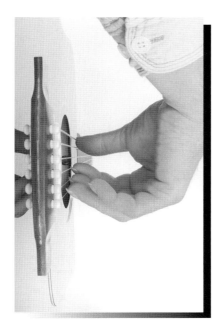
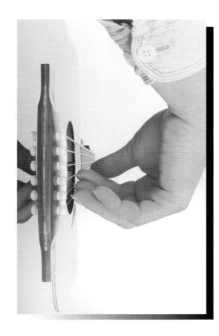
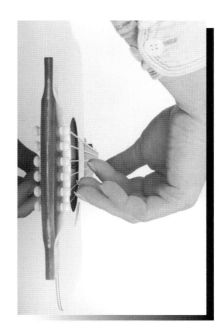
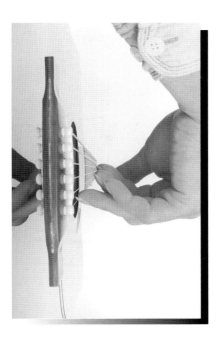
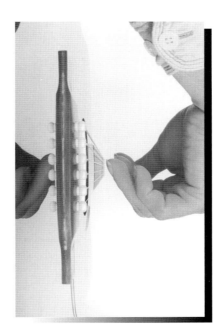
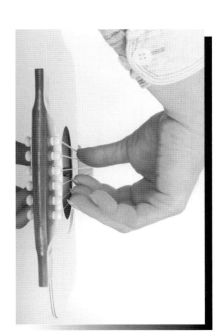

Preparatory Exercise For The Arpeggio

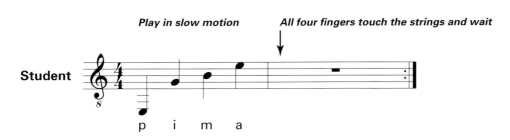

Play in slow motion   *All four fingers touch the strings and wait*

Student

p   i   m   a

Now you're ready for the next piece. The right hand movements are the same as in the exercise. However, the thumb doesn't only play the E-string, but the A-string as well.

Below The Ocean

By now, you should know the next song "I Play Guitar" well. This time the accompanying chords are not strummed but arpeggiated. The thumb plays all three low strings. The left-hand movements are the same as in the previous version. The melody can be played by your teacher or by another student.

I Play Guitar
(3rd Version)

2. THE BLUES

Before you turn to the next piece, we would like you to put your guitar aside. For the first time we will now get to know a music style that has impacted pop and rock music like no other: the blues.

Robert Johnson

What's Blues?

Well, it would fill books to tell you the whole story.
But here's at least some facts ...

The blues originates in the songs of the black slaves that were carried off from Africa to America during the 18th and 19th century.
Singing the blues was these people's way to express their pain and homesickness. To have the blues means to be sad and miserable.

Bessie Smith, one of the great female blues singers, sang: *"Nobody knows you when you're down and out."*

Blues-guitarist John Lee Hooker sings: *"I've got the blues so bad, it's hard to keep me from cryin'."*

And in *"Trouble in Mind Blues"*, the lyrics say that *"When you see me laughing, I'm laughing just to keep me from crying."*

From the cotton fields, the blues entered the American cities. Influenced by the white American music, it started to change. Finally, Rock'n'Roll and pop music evolved ...

Even today you will find that any serious pop musician admires the blues and regards it their musical root. A great example is the British guitarist Eric Clapton, in whose music the blues has always played a major role
And what would the Rolling Stones be without the blues ...?

Our First Blues

Just like every blues, "Deep Down Blues" consists of three chords. In this case, the chords are E-minor, A-minor and B7. You have already learned the fingering for Em and Am. We can simplify these chords for "Deep Down Blues" because we don't want to strum all six strings. So, here are the two new shapes of Em and Am.

Em

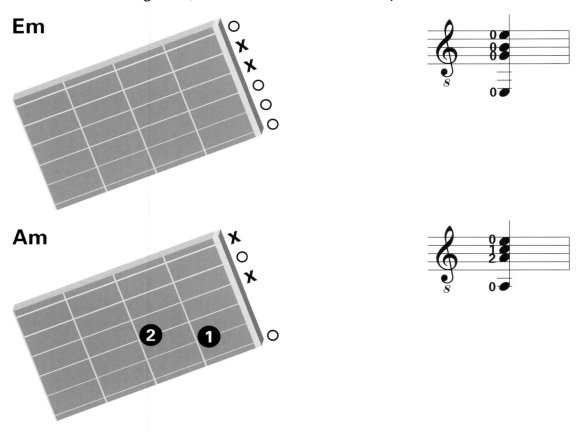

Am

The third chord is called B7. As it is always preceded by E-minor in this tune and the left hand is not needed for E-minor in this case, you can prepare the fingering for B7 in the air. Bring your fingers as close to their expected position on the fingerboard as you possibly can.

B7

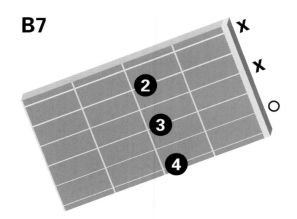

Did you notice anything?

When taking a close look at the notation next to the B7-chord, you should notice this new, strange sign occuring there. It looks like a piece of a picketfence.

Musicians call this accidental "sharp". It tells the guitarist that the note before which it occurs is raised by a half step or one fret. Go back to page 64. That's where we explained in detail what half and whole steps are.

So, in our new chord B7 the sharp raises the tone F

f'

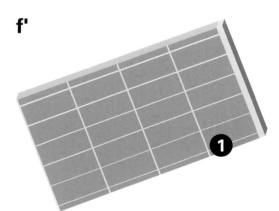

to **F-sharp**.

fis'

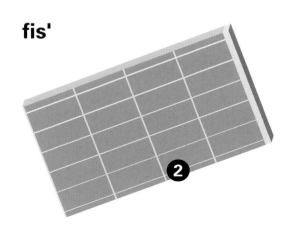

Deep Down Blues
(1st Version)

3. ALL AT ONCE: HOW TO PLAY BARRED CHORDS

A "Classic" Tune On The Guitar: "The House Of The Rising Sun"

The next song has probably been played by guitarists more than any other one. Whenever somebody picks up a guitar at a campfire or a beach-party, they most likely play this song, too. Nobody knows who wrote it. It comes from North America and has become a traditional, a folk song. Bob Dylan made this tune popular; it can be heard on his first record. In Europe, it became famous in the 1960s through an electric guitar version recorded by the British pop band "The Animals".

Six-Eight Time

All the tunes and pieces we have played so far are in common time (4/4). There are many other types of times, such as six-eight time. When a song is written in six-eight time, like "The House Of The Rising Sun", each measure consists of six eighth notes. Let's practice this with the simple E-minor chord that we used in the previous piece "Deep Down Blues".

In order to be able to play the 6/8 time pattern, we need to extend our arpeggio pattern "p i m a" by two more picks. Count **1** 2 3 **4** 5 6 ..., play the first and fourth note slightly louder than the others and you'll be fine ...

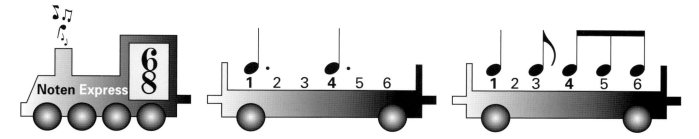

Barred Chords
A New Fingering Technique

In order to play "The House Of The Rising Sun" we need to learn a new fingering technique, the **barring** of chords. This technique allows us to lay the left-hand first finger across two, three or even six strings at the same time. (You can't bar more strings, of course, because your guitar has only six.) For example:

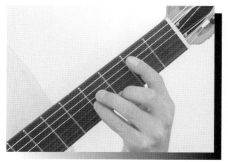

"The House Of The Rising Sun" uses a new chord that requires this new barring technique. It's called **F-Major**. The first finger bars across **two** strings.

F

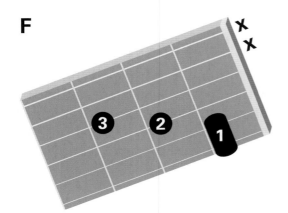

Before the notes C and F you can see a bracket. This bracket is always used to indicate that the strings need to be **barred**.

As this technique is not that easy to employ, you might have to practice for a while before you actually master it. We would like to help you to approach your goal step by step with the following tips.

While going through these steps, make sure that your left-hand thumb is across from the first fretwire at all times. Hold it straight like this:

Don't hold it like this:

Step 1: A short preparatory exercise **without** your guitar. Switch back and forth between these two finger postures:

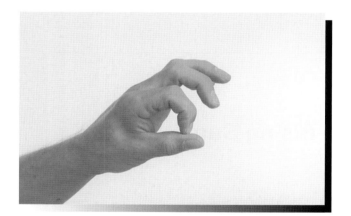
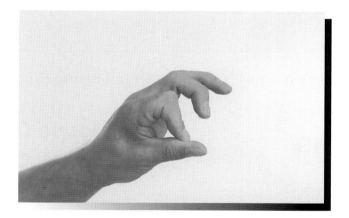

Step 2: Pick the open strings B and E first. Lay your first finger across these two strings. You can now hear the tones C and F.

Step 3: We're approaching the complete F-major chord now (see photo of F-Major chord on page 114). Place your 3rd finger on F on the D-string and your 2nd finger on A on the G-string. The 1. finger bars across the other two strings, as described in step 2.

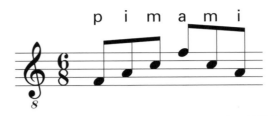

Be careful! The barring technique is not a question of pressure. In the beginning it is most likely that your new F-Major chord doesn't sound too good. Certain tones might rattle or sound muffled. However, trying to make things better by putting more pressure on the strings is wrong and will have the opposite effect. What you need to do instead is have a little patience and keep on practising the above steps 1 to 3. It often takes only minor changes in the finger position to create a much better sound. Every guitarist has to experiment until they find their **own** way to bar the strings; this is because every hand is different! We, the authors of this book, both have a vivid memory of our problems with the barring technique. It takes some time, that's all!

Let's get to "The House Of the Rising Sun" now.

The House Of The Rising Sun
Melody: Trad.

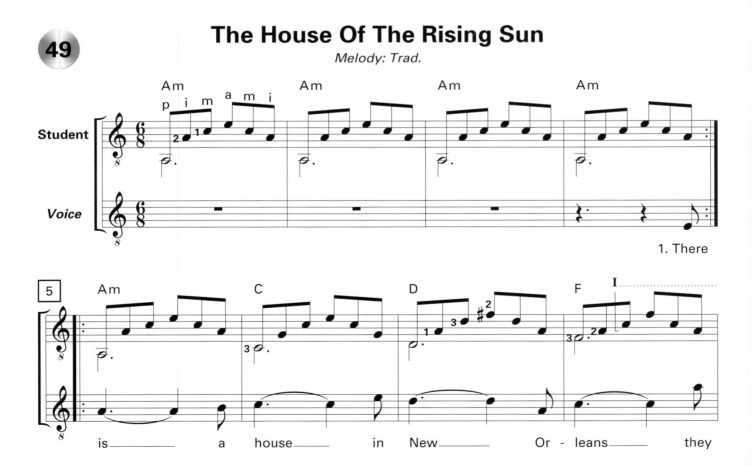

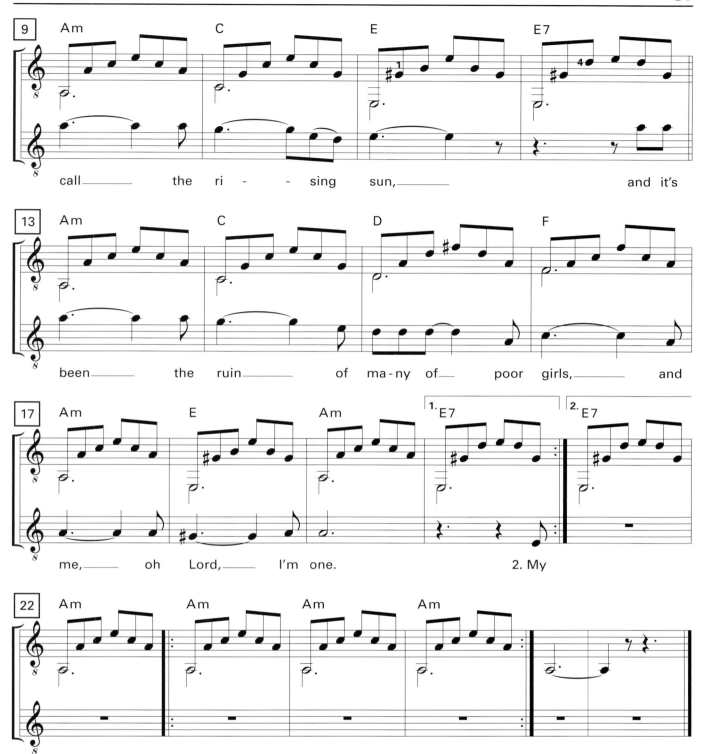

9 Am / C / E / E7

call___ the ri - - sing sun,___ and it's

13 Am / C / D / F

been___ the ruin___ of ma-ny of___ poor girls,___ and

17 Am / E / Am / 1. E7 / 2. E7

me,___ oh Lord,___ I'm one.   2. My

22 Am / Am / Am / Am

2. My mother was a tailor,
   she sewed those new blue jeans
   my husband he's a gambling man,
   drinks down in New Orleans.

3. Go tell my baby sister,
   not to do what I have done
   to live the life in sin and misery
   in the house of the rising sun.

4. One foot on the platform,
   the other's on the train,
   I'm going back to New Orleans,
   to wear that ball and chain.

5. I'm going back to New Orleans,
   my race is almost run,
   I'm going to spent the rest of my live
   beneath that rising sun.

Flats

We have already talked about one type of accidental. Sharps raise the tones that they precede by one half step. In contrast to this, **flats lower** the following tone by a half step. The symbol for a flat is ♭. The first lowered tone we get to know is B-flat. It is a half step below B and is played on the third fret of the G-string.

b-flat

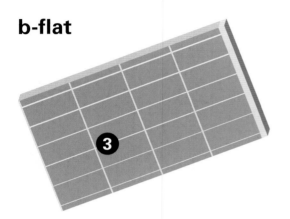

The new chord **G-minor** contains the tone B-flat. This chord is barred; however, this time the first finger bars over **three** strings.

Gm

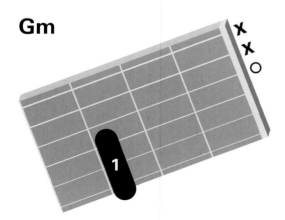

The second new chord is **D-minor**.

Dm

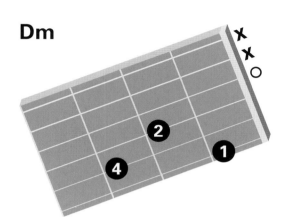

 The D on the B-string is played with the **fourth, not with the third finger**.

The new chord **D-minor7** is barred as well. It is closely related to the F-Major chord. Use the fingering of the F-Major chord; lift the third finger and play the D-string open.

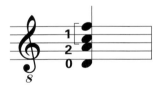

Dm7

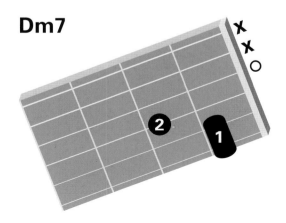

For the next tune we need another chord that is fairly easy to play: **Am7**.

Am7

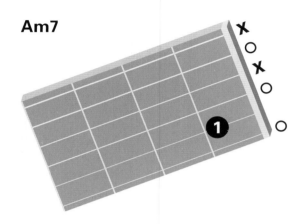

Let's take you to "Acapulco" now.
Mexico is a hot place and we hope you won't be sweating too much.

50

Acapulco

4. IT WORKS BETTER WITH TWO: ALTERNATE STROKE

You've probably been wondering whether in the long run it is enough to use only one finger for picking a melody on the strings. Of course it's not and that is why we're going to learn the **alternate stroke** now.

But what is this anyway?

Well, so far we have played all melodies, i.e. each single tone, with the thumb only. That was fine and we're still going to use this type of picking in the future as well. However, this method is limited when it comes to playing longer and faster melody sequences. In such cases it is better to use alternate plucking, i.e. we use **two** fingers instead of **one**.

Alternate plucking is a very, very important technique. As we want to learn it properly, we have to invest some time.

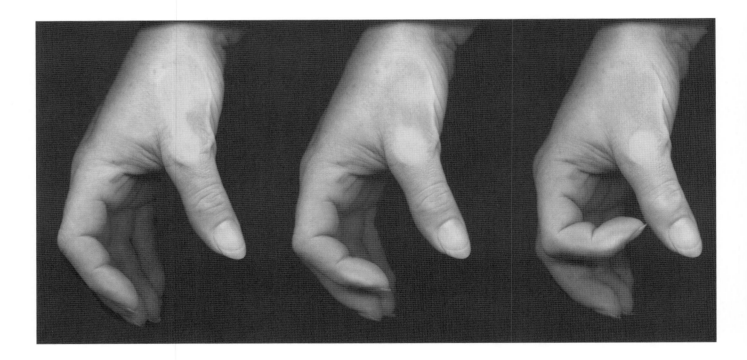

The movement your finger has to carry out for this picking technique resembles that of a bulldozer.

The three joints of your finger curl inwards towards the palm of your hand just like the three teeth of a bulldozer shovel. Your hand has the shape of a "C" that is getting smaller and smaller.

C   C   c

If the bulldozer shovel is driven too deeply into the ground, it will get stuck! The same will happen to your fingertip if you put it too far in between the strings.

If the teeth of the bulldozer shovel have the wrong shape, it will be hard to work efficiently with it. The same applies to your fingernails. When they are too long or when they are split, they will get stuck in the strings. The simplest solution is to trim the nails short.
However, it is better to take care of them and file them correctly. In our Appendix you can read everything you need to know about this.

Let's get back to the guitar. We exercise this stroke with i (the index or 1st finger) playing the open G-string. p is resting loosely on the low E-string, m on the B-string and a on the E-string.

First Finger Stroke

So far, we've only talked about the first finger (i).
But what was the title of this chapter again? "It works better with two". Correct. And for this reason we're now adding the second finger as a partner for the first one. It does everything the same way the first one does it. And again, just like in the previous exercise, we rest the fingers that aren't picking on the strings we're not playing (p on the E-string, i on the G-string and a on the E-string.)

Second Finger Stroke

Student

When i and m **take turns** in picking the strings, we have reached our goal: That's what we call **alternate stroke**!

Before we try this, we'd like you to visualize something that, at first sight, doesn't have anything to do with guitar playing. Take a look at what our legs do when we're walking:

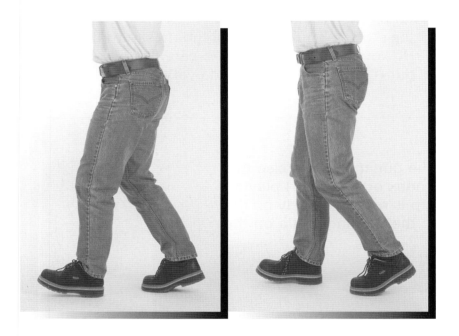

When we're walking, our legs constantly **take turns** as well. One leg is ahead, the other is behind. That's the only way to walk. Try it!

Now this is how it looks when our two fingers are "walking":

Let's now practice the "walking", the alternate stroke on the guitar. Let your thumb rest lightly on the low E-string.

Alternate Stroke On The G- And B-String

Now here's the final step: We're "walking" on one string.

Alternate Stroke On The G-String

Guitarists call this alternate plucking technique **tirando**, by the way.

 There's another important thing to say about the tirando: It actually does make a difference whether you start a melody with the first finger (i), or with the second finger (m)! Many melodies can be played more easily and smoothly if you switch to another string with the correct finger. In this book it is always indicated with which finger you should start.

Now we would like to use our new technique to play a song that we already encountered in chapter 1 of section B: "Lullaby". All tones of this tune are on the D-string. Start the tirando with i.

Lullaby
(2. version)

You know the next song "By The Riverside" as well. (We played it in chapter 3 of section B.) All tones are on the B-string and we start plucking with m.

By The Riverside
(2nd Version)

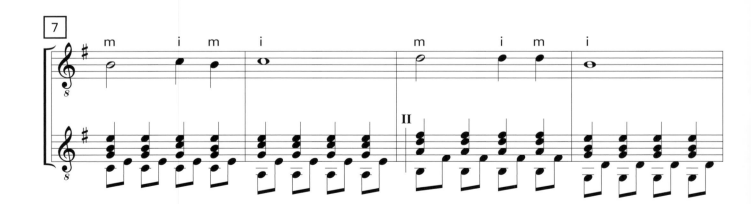

Before you continue with the next chapter, which introduces some classical music, we'd like to encourage you to try the classical sitting position. Although you could probably master the following pieces in other playing positions as well, we still think it makes total sense to play classical music in the classical position. Don't you agree?

(By the way, we, the authors, do the same thing. We change the way we're holding the guitar with the musical style.)

5. GOOD OLD STUFF – CLASSICAL MUSIC

What's classical music?

We briefly touched the subject of classical music in chapter 3, section B when we played Beethoven's piece "Ode To Joy" (An Die Freude). We'd like to explore the world of classical music with a little more depth now.

Let's find out first what the words "classic" and "classical" actually mean. Put the guitar away for a minute and continue reading …

We are surrounded by things that carry the attribute "classic", such as the look of clothes, the shape of a car, the scent of a perfume or even the design of a coffee-machine. Something that carries the label "classic" is considered to be timeless, permanent, neverending. The same is true for the classical period, its music and literature, which have survived over the centuries. They seem immortal and timeless.

Guitar virtuoso

In music, the years from 1780 and 1830 are called "The Classical Period". The most famous composers of this time are Joseph Haydn, Wolfgang Amadeus Mozart and Ludwig van Beethoven. But even music that was written long before or after this time is often referred to as "classical".

Classical music combines the simple and traditional musical language of folk songs and dances with the masterly craft of the composers. This way a musical world full of great harmony and power was created: songs, symphonies, concertos, chamber music and guitar music, too.

The "Allegro" by Mauro Giuliani, which we're going to play at the end of this chapter, is one of the original compositions from this time, a classical guitar-piece.

Joseph Haydn

The first piece in this chapter is by Robert Schumann. It is taken from his "Kinderszenen", a collection of piano pieces. You will see that it sounds wonderful on guitar as well. Its title is "Von fremden Ländern und Menschen".

Robert Schumann, composer and pianist, was born in Zwickau, Germany, in 1810, and died in Bonn in 1856

The Dotted Eighth Note

In this piece, we'll get to know a new rhythmic element that consists of two types of notes we haven't encountered yet: a dotted eighth note and a sixteenth note. How does that work?

You probably remember how we introduced the eighth note by cutting a quarter note into two identical halves. Now if we do the same thing with an eighth note, what are we going to get? Two sixteenth notes, of course!

Two eighth notes make four sixteenth notes:

By combining the first three sixteenth notes into one, we have a dotted eighth note. One sixteenth note is left over at the end.

A good way to practice this is by counting. (Every 1/16 note receives a count.)

Start slowly.

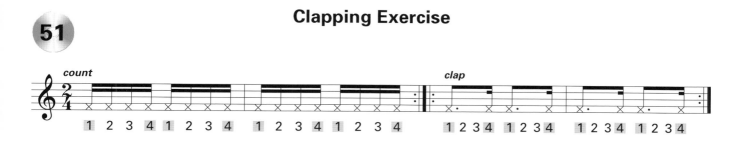

Now clap your hands on the "1" and the "4" while you continue counting.

This exercise is on the CD, too. We count to "4" four times; then the clapping sets in. After a while, the whole thing becomes faster ...

Clapping Exercise

51

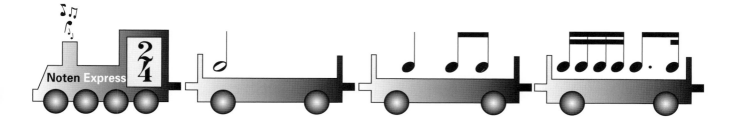

You would have probably noticed yourself that **2/4** is indicated directly after the clef in the following piece. Two-four time is closely related with common time (4/4). The difference between the two is that common time (4/4) has a strong emphasis on the first count and a minor one on the third one; this one doesn't occur in 2/4, of course, because there's only two quarters in each measure.

Oh, before we forget ... Robert Schumann's piece uses a strange sign that resembles an eye. It is called **fermata** and tells us to hold the note above which it is written. This way, the steadily flowing tempo of the music is briefly stopped at specific notes.

Fermata:

Von fremden Ländern und Menschen

Melody: Robert Schumann (+1856)

The next piece takes us to a completely different and very special musical world. It was written by one of the "craziest" composers ever. Besides "normal" tones from "regular" instruments, he also used the clicking of type-writers or gunshots in his music. Sometimes, however, his music can be simple and quiet, almost empty. One of his typical statements is: *"Before I sit down to notate a musical work, I walk around it with myself a couple times."* Welcome to the world of **Eric Satie**.

Eric Satie, the "craziest" composer of the world,
born 1866 in Honfleur, France, died 1925 in Paris

Gymnopédie (the piece received this odd title by the composer) is written in **3/4 time**. Besides 4/4 time, 3/4 is the most common type of time. The most famous example for 3/4 time is the waltz. In 3/4, the "1" is more or less emphasized; in Satie's piece the "1" receives only a minor emphasis.

Play slowly and calmly....

Gymnopédie

Melody: Eric Satie

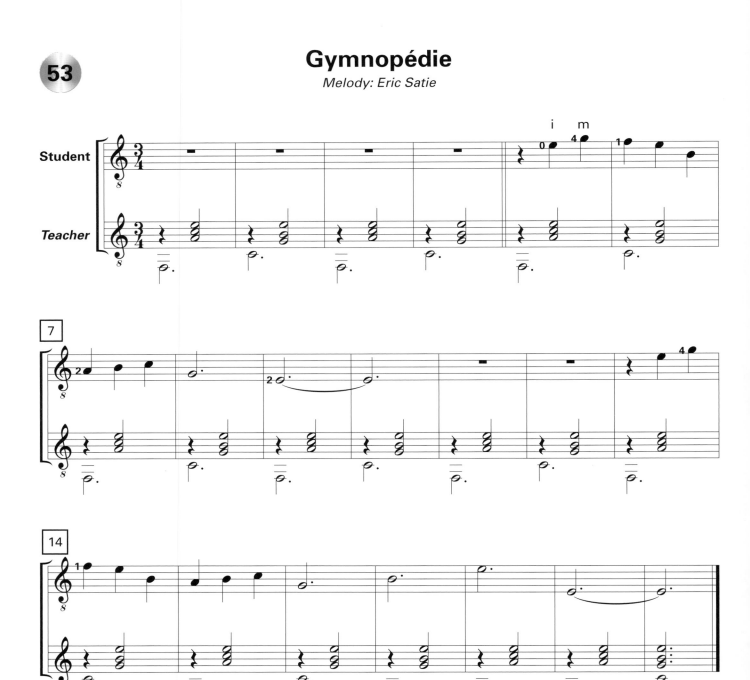

Loud And Soft ...

In the next piece we would like to try something new: how to play certain melody parts louder or softer. Musicians call this **"dynamics"** and, as usual, they've invented symbols for these as well. The three most important ones are: **forte** (= loud), **mezzoforte** (= medium) and **piano** (= soft).

You know this from CD-players or stereos.

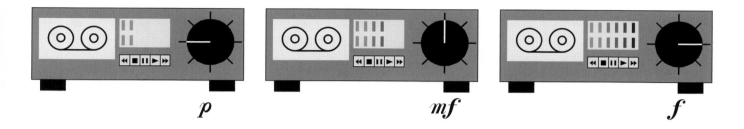

In the following piece we will practice loud and soft tones. To make it easy, we're using the signs $\boldsymbol{f}$ (forte), $\boldsymbol{mf}$ (mezzoforte) and $\boldsymbol{p}$ (piano). These abbreviations are indicated in the music and tell us when to play loud and when to play soft.

Try this with the tune "Waldhorn". You´ll create an echo by changing betweeen playing forte and piano. At first you can hear the Waldhorn loud and clearly, then it reverberates softly from the mountains.

By the way, "Waldhorn" originates from the collection "Notenbuch fuer Wolfgang" from 1762. Leopold Mozart put this collection together for his son Wolfgang Amadeus so that he was able to practice the piano properly.

The fermata that we know from Schumann's "Von fremden Ländern und Menschen" occurs here as well.

The Waldhorn

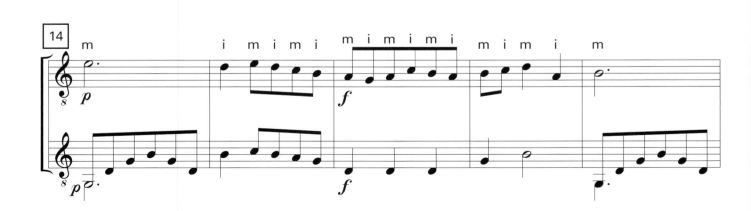

Our next piece was written by a composer who is widely regarded as the greatest composer of all times: Johann Sebastian Bach.

Johann Sebastian Bach, born 1685 in Eisenach, died 1750 in Leipzig. His legacy to us are more than 1.000 compositions.

During his lifetime, Bach was not an acknowledged writer and later fell into oblivion for almost 100 years. Today, however, he is considered to be one of the most famous masters of music. The following piece is one of his numerous little studies for the piano. It sounds nice on the guitar as well. It's a minuet, a calm dance in 3/4 time. At Bach's time, the minuet was the most popular dance of the aristocracy.

Two New Tones And A New Fret

F-sharp. This note is our first one on the 4th fret. We play it with the 4th finger.

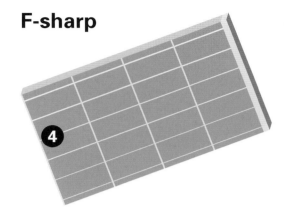

F-sharp

C-sharp.

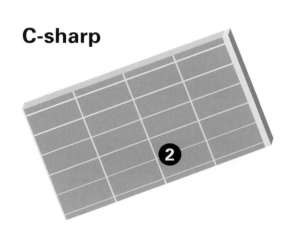

C-sharp

Attention: In measure 20 it is better to play A with the 1st finger. Then the 2nd finger doesn't need to leap!

55

Minuet

Play It One More Time
More Songs To Practice Alternate Plucking

Of course, we can play all the melodies from section B of this book by using tirando, alternate plucking. Use the following selection to practice the tirando:

Page	CD-Track	Title	Part(s):
100	45	Up And Down	student
98	44	Darkness	student
97	43	Funk The A	student
89	21	You Are Gone (2nd Version)	student
88	40	Friends At The Sea	student
84	38	Ode To Joy (An die Freude)	student 1, student 2
82	37	Without Words	student

6. IT'S ONLY ROCK'N ROLL – BUT WE LIKE IT!

The previous chapter was quite classical: We played little pieces by Johann Sebastian Bach, Leopold Mozart, Robert Schumann and Eric Satie. And we learned a new picking technique as well, the tirando, which enables us to play classical pieces fluently and smoothly.

For rock and pop music there is also a right-hand technique that allows a more fluent and quicker playing than the thumb picking: **alternate picking** using a pick or plectrum. We already know the pick from section A of this book where we used it to strum chords. When doing this, **the two sides of the pick automatically take turns for the downstroke and upstroke.**

This is the foundation of alternate picking However, we don't strike **several** strings with the pick. Just a single **one** at first.

Of course, we need to slightly change our strumming technique and hand posture from the ones used for striking chords:

Now we're striking the strings not with a **big** movement of the forearm anymore, but with a **small** twist.

This automatically creates the alternate picking with the sides of the pick taking constant turns. Only thumb and first finger are needed to hold the pick.

The other fingers hang loosely in a more or less curled manner. It is also OK to rest the pinkie lightly on the guitar top. And we really mean LIGHTLY because it might move a little bit. Find out for yourself if this helps you to play more securely.

 In any case, the pick should be held loosely between the thumb and first finger, but tight enough to keep it from flying away during your playing.

Also keep in mind: There's no such thing as the **one and only** correct posture for playing with a pick. You will have to find out with time what posture works best for you! Note the tips above in any case!

We already know the signs for the downstroke (V) and the upstroke (⊓) from strumming chords.

Exercise

Apply this exercise to all other strings as well.

The following pieces and songs have already occured in section B of this book. We will now use them to practice alternate picking with the pick. Start every piece with a down-stroke and remember to **always alternate downstroke** and **upstroke.**

Page	CD-Track	Title	Part (s)
125	25	Lullaby (2nd Version)	student
65	26	Belas Traum	student
126	31	By The Riveside (2nd Version)	student
68	32	Native Dance (1st Version)	student 1
78	34	Summer Dance	student
108	36	I Play Guitar (2nd Version)	student
82	37	Without Words	student

Let's Improvise ...

Once again we would like to return to the blues. The second version of "Deep Down Blues" has the same chord progression as the first one; however, now you don't play the accompaniment but the guitar solo!

Blues music is usually **improvised** and not played with sheet music. Improvising means to play certain tones freely and spontaneously.

With the following five tones we can improvise to the three chords used in our blues tune (Em, Am and B7):

5-Note Exercise

If your CD player has a balance knob, turn it all the way to the right. Now you can improvise to the music played by your band.

 **Avoid** playing **too many notes**!

Deep Down Blues
(2nd Version)

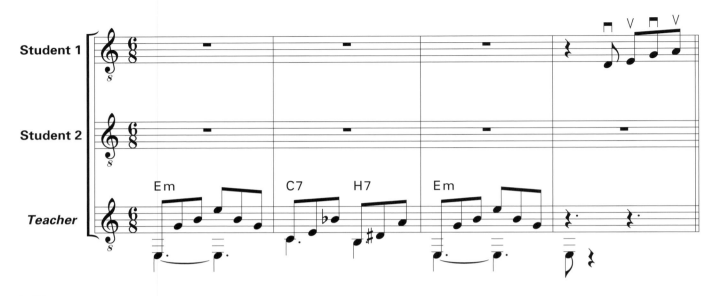

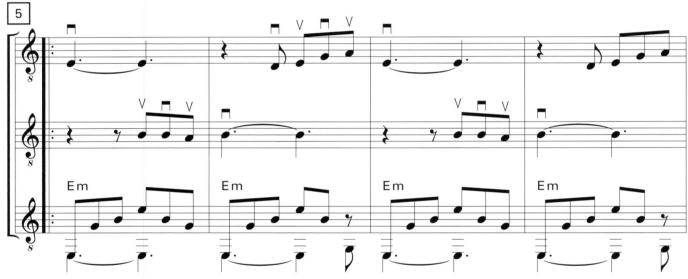

Note: The melodies of the first and second part sound great together as well.

Power Chords

We're now turning to a techique that is commonly used in rock and pop music: **power chords**. The name already tells you how powerful these chords sound although they only consist of **two** notes! They are played with the pick and close to the guitar bridge. **Always hit two strings** with one **downstroke**! This way, you can create a rock sound even on a nylon-string guitar.

For the left hand, all power chords are the same: **If you can play one, you can play them all**. For the next "power piece" we use four of these chords that are always written with a "5" next to the chord name.

 For the first time, the left hand is now leaving the familiar first three frets: The first finger moves up to the fifth fret. It's not necessary for you to learn the name of the tones by heart at this point; however, it is important to know the location of the power chords on the fingerboard, i.e. their so-called **position**. The position is determined by the fret where the first finger is placed! If it is placed on the fifth fret, you are playing in the V. position; if it is placed on the third, you are in the III. position and so forth.
(Positions are indicated by Roman numerals.)

When moving from one power chord to another, we don't completely lift the fingers off the strings! They slide up and down the strings like on a railway.

A5

G5

F5

E5

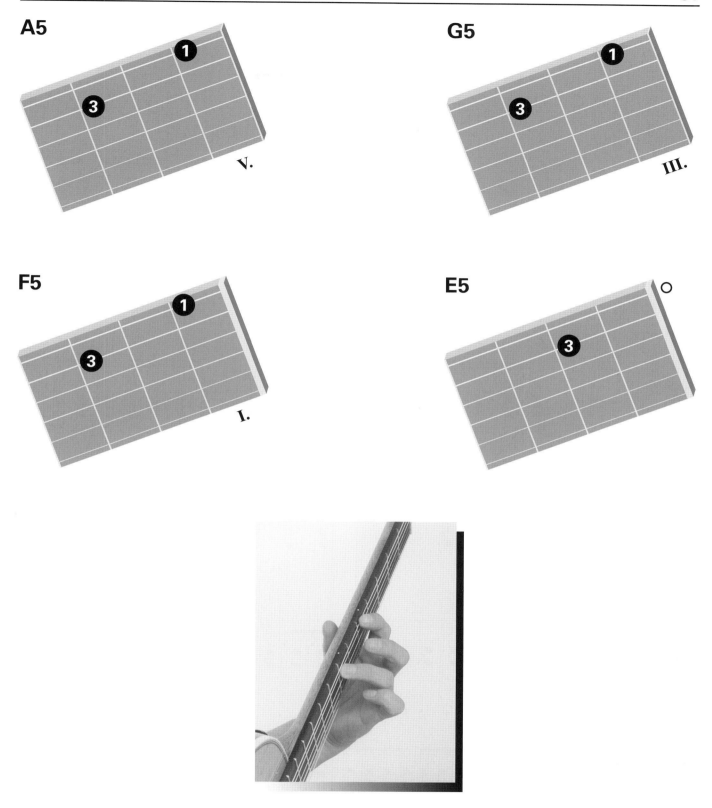

The chords are played with the first and third finger. Many guitarists use the fourth finger instead of the third one. Try and find out what feels better for you. Of course, it is the best to master both fingerings.

Your Power

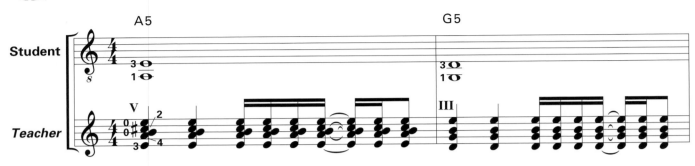

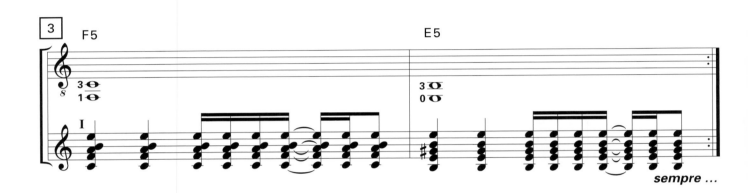

sempre …

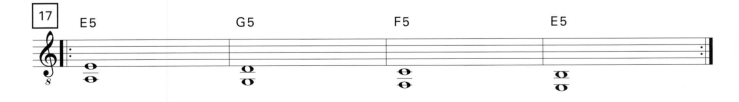

If you fiddle around with these chords for a while, you will soon develop your own chord progressions. These chords sound great as well on the A- and D-string or on the D- and G-string.

Have fun!

For the conclusion of this chapter, we picked something special:
A hot rumba with a rock beat!
The rumba originates in Afro-Cuban music and the Spanish flamenco; but its rhythm and characteristic chord progressions are perfectly fit to "go rock".

"The Sunny Side" uses three the chord progessions that are typical for the rumba:

In measures 1 to 17:

Em, D7, C, B7

You have already learned these chords. However, we add another tone to B7 (see page 110 on the bottom): D-sharp, which is played by the first finger.

B7

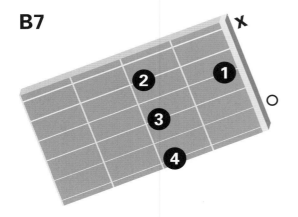

In measures 19 to 25:

Am, G, F, E7

You know these chords, too. Sometimes E is played instead of the E7-chord.

In measures 27 to 35:

Am, (A7), Dm, E7

Nothing new either. The A7-chord is in parantheses because it is often omitted, too.

The Rumba Stroke

Let's now talk about the right hand. This is the rumba's typical rhythm pattern:

Make the hand movement for the strokes that are shown in parentheses without actually touching the strings (air stroke)!

The trick is to play the important beat on the **two-and** with an upstroke; and that's the only way to do it!

Finally, polish your playing by striking the **one** and the **two-and** slightly louder (accent).

We recorded your guitar part with a pick (that is not too hard), something a real Flamenco-guitarist would never do! But because you're not familiar with these special Flamenco strumming techniques, it's OK for now to use the pick.

The Sunny Side

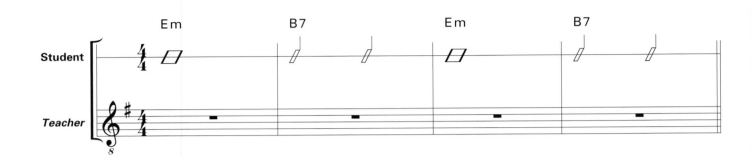

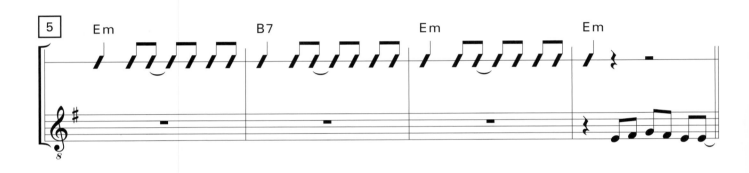

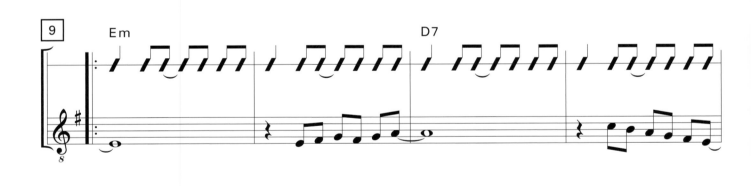

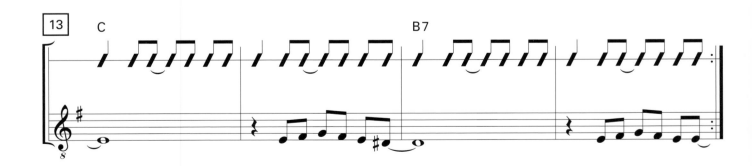

7. YOUR FIRST SOLO-PIECES

Up to this point, you always needed your teacher or the CD to make music; you needed an accompaniment and played along with other musicians.

Another way to make music is **solo-playing**. You've learned enough by now to be able to start doing this as well.

We've chosen two very different pieces for this: One comes from the world of classical music and the other from pop music. We start with the pop song because we already know it well. We have played both the chords and the melody before individually but not **together**. Now we put together what belongs together: melody and accompaniment.

There is an easy way to distinguish melody and accompaniment in the musical notation: The stems of the melody notes point upward; the stems of the accompanying notes point downward. (Once in a while there are some exceptions.) It may now appear as if all these notes don't fit into one measure. But when you count the time values of each individual **part**, everything is fine again: The total time value of each part fills one measure. This means when playing solo, you play two or more parts simultaneously – you play **harmonized music** or **multiple-voice music**.

We already know most of the techniques needed for solo-playing. But now we will employ them all at once. Thumb stroke and tirando for the right hand, chord fingering and melody playing for the left hand.

However, there's one new technique used in the next piece: the simultaneous plucking with different fingers. Various combinations of p, i, m, and a are applied.

Guitarists call this **"closed position"**.

The patterns needed for "You are gone" are:

Preparatory Exercise 1

Preparatory Exercise 2

You Are Gone

(3rd Version)

With the next piece, we once again return to the world of classical music. And this time we really do because this "Allegro" by Mauro Giuliani is an original piece for the classical guitar.

Mauro Giuliano, born in 1781 in Bisceglie (Southern Italy), died 1829 in Vienna.
He was one of the great guitar virtuosos of the classical period.

Let's look at the left hand first: It is grabbing chords, in this case five different ones. Three of these are already known: Am, Dm and E. They have been slightly changed here and sometimes they have a different note in the bass. The two new fingerings are **E7** (we played an E7-chord before but we need a different fingering here) and **Esus4**.

Esus4 sounds quite dangerous but it really isn't …

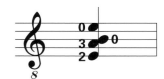

Esus4

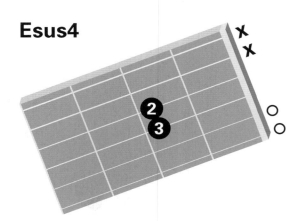

Now let's turn to the new E7-chord. It contains a new tone: The G of the open G-string is raised to G-sharp.

E7

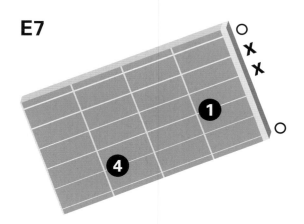

It is used with B as the bass note as well:

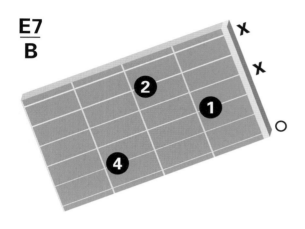

That's it for the left hand. Let's now turn to the right hand. We've worked with **arpeggios** numerous times; here's a new pattern applied to the chord Am:

Note the small lines in the measure. Keep the finger placed on the string for the two notes connected by this line. This makes it easier for you to change the fingering. Start with the following preparatory exercise:

Preparatory Exercise 1

Also note: In some measures of "Allegro", the bass notes are not half notes but quarter notes! This means the respective bass tones have to be stopped or as the guitatists call it, **muted**. The string is muted with the right-hand thumb: Place it on the bass-string when the third finger (a) plucks its string. This is not easy. So let's practice it with the open strings first:

Preparatory Exercise 2

Thumb is placed on the fifth string

Let's now practice this muting technique for our piece "Allegro":

Preparatory Exercise 3

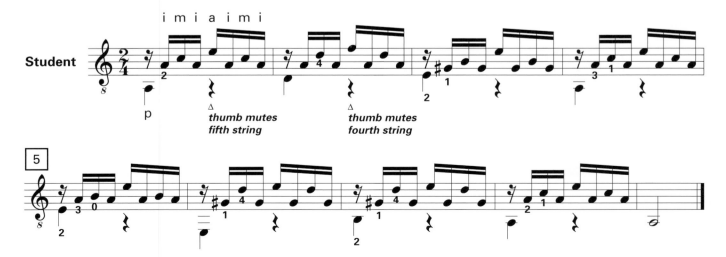

Giuliani's "Allegro" uses another fingerstyle technique: the alternate picking of thumb and first finger. Practice this on the open strings first ...

Preparatory Exercise 4

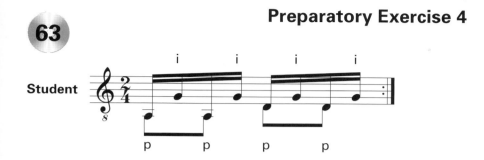

... and now with the fingering used in the piece:

Preparatory Exercise 5

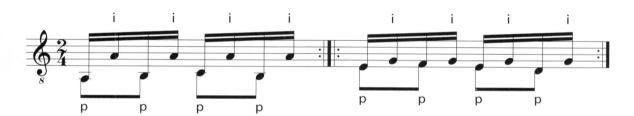

OK, now we can finally turn to "Allegro". But what does "Allegro" actually mean? The word is Italian as are most musical terms. The literal translation is "cheerful" and "amusing". So, that's how we want to play Giuliani's piece. Don't play it too slowly because for musicians "allegro" also means "fast".

Allegro

Melody: Mauro Giuliani

8. FINALE

Take care and see you soon!

Here you are: You've arrived at the final piece of this guitar book. It's sure been a long road that we walked together and you've learned a lot on the way: How to accompany songs and play melodies and your first solo-pieces; you've learned folk, rock and pop songs and little classical pieces; and you played your first blues ... By now, you are familiar with various basic techniques needed to play the guitar and to make music. And yet, this is just the beginning of the journey. You've only slightly opened the door to your new musical world and there's so much more to discover. There's a lot you've been able to pack in your suitcase by now ... We wish you much fun, joy and success on this trip to "your new world". Stay patient and calm while going there.

Now back to work one more time ...

Our final piece "Concertino" applies all the important techniques you've learned by now: How to strike and arppegiate chords and how to play melodies with a pick or by employing the tirando-technique.
One little thing is new: The time signature changes in the middle of the tune. We start with common time (4/4), switch to 6/8 time and return to 4/4. Pay attention to these transitions; they shouldn't be hard for you.

The four new chords E, D, G and Dmaj7 are displayed in the chord overview on page 182. They won't be a problem for you either.

Because this is a very special day, you won't be accompanied by a band consisting of only drums, bass and keyboards – we have added a lot of violins and a brass section as well ...

Concertino

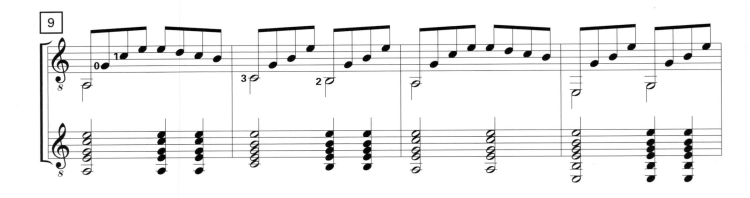

Appendix

THE TABLATURE

A Different Way To Notate Guitar Music

Hand-written original of the Chaconne from the Partita C-Major by Johann Anton Losy von Losinthal (around 1650-1721). The original manuscript can be found at the library of the Prague University.

At this time we would like to point out a notation technique that is commonly applied by folk and rock guitarists: tablature.

This way of notating music is very old. The first pieces for stringed instruments which were printed in a tablature originate in the beginning of the 16th century; and it was a common method to notate music until the 18th century.
Then tablatures were replaced by music notation in staffs. You might wonder why you should bother learning about tablatures after regular music notation took its place.

Well, in some areas tablatures are still used to the present day. As mentioned above this is true for folk musicians or lute-players and increasingly for rock and pop musicians as well. This should be reason enough for a guitarist to learn reading tablatures. As you are an experienced guitarist yourself now and it is only a matter of time before you'll come across a guitar book using tablatures, we want you to be prepared.

Six Strings = Six Lines

In contrast to the staff which consists of five lines, the tablature has six lines. These lines represent the **six guitar strings**; the bottom line represents the low E-string and the top line represents the high E-string.

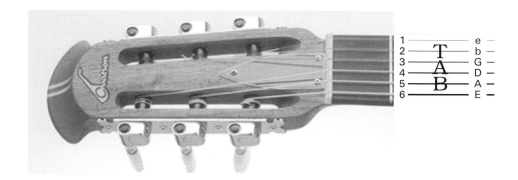

This is logical and simple, isn't it? The next steps are easy, too: We write numbers on the lines (strings) to indicate which fret you have to play. If "1" is written on the top line, for example, you have to play the first fret of the high E-string.

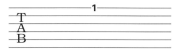

Now you've played a note that you know as F. Tablature certainly presents you with the same tones as the staff notation; it just has a different way to display them.

When a tone is on the 2. fret, we write "2" in the tablature and so forth: 3 for the third fret, 4 for the fourth etc.

Here are some examples:

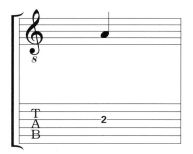
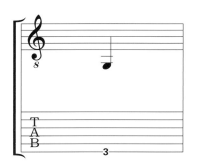
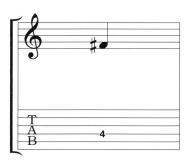

A "0" on a line indicates that the string is to be played open, of course.

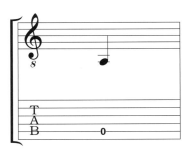

The time values of the tones are the same as in the staff notation. The stems usually point downwards.

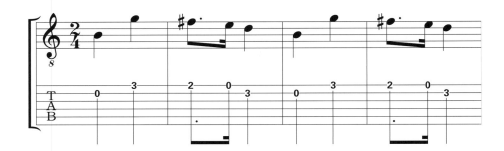

A minor disadvantage of tablature is the fact that half and whole notes cannot be distinguished. You know that these types of notes have hollow heads which cannot be displayed in the tablature numbers. However, this is not too big of a deal because most guitar books with tablature show the staff notation as well. There you can check the exact time values. Everything else, such as measures, ties, dottings, beams, up- and downstroke of the right hand, is used the same way.

Before we write down the entire melody line of Schumann's "Von fremden Ländern und Menschen", let's take a brief look at the way chords are represented in tablatures. It works like staff notation as well: Numbers (tones) notated in a vertical line above each other are played simultaneously. For example:

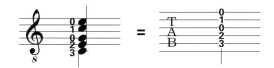

Now try to write down Robert Schumann's melody in the tablature. We're sure it won't be difficult for you.

Von fremden Ländern und Menschen

If you would like to practice reading and writing tablature some more, you can do so with every piece in this book.

GENERAL TIPS FOR THE GUITAR

Purchase

If you don't have a guitar yet or you don't have a good one and you would like to buy one or get one as a gift, there's a few things to keep in mind.

Check these three issues:

1. Does the guitar have a straight neck?

To check this, you have to look down the guitar neck as shown on the photo below:

The neck must be **absolutely straight!**

2. Do the strings have the proper distance to the fingerboard?

This can be checked by controlling the distance of the strings to the fret wires as shown on the photos below:

If the strings are **too high** above the fret wires, the instrument is **not appropriate** for a beginner!

Bad!

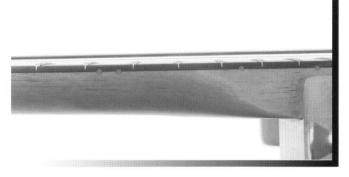
Good!

3. Are the tuning machines working correctly?

Make sure that the tuning keys can be turned **easily and without making noise**.

How To Treat The Guitar

Here are a few things your guitar definitely doesn't like:

Rough treatment. When you don't play, place the instrument somewhere safe so that it cannot **fall down**.

Bad!

Good!

Extreme Heat Or Cold. It's harmful for your guitar to leave it in the sun or inside a car trunk during summer ... And it's of course just as bad to expose it to low temperatures for a longer time in winter. **Very dry air** does harm to your instrument, too. Heated rooms with bad ventilation tend to have dry air. And it's better anyway for you and your instrument to keep the air **not too dry**. Air out the room.

How To Change Strings

The strings of your guitar cannot be used forever. After a while, they start losing their brilliance and it's time to put new strings on. Do this about twice a year. Here are some tips on how to change strings.

On a nylon-string guitar, it's important to tie the strings **correctly**. This is what you do on the bridge:

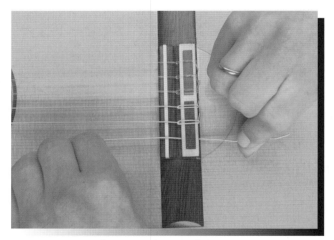

Insert the string ...

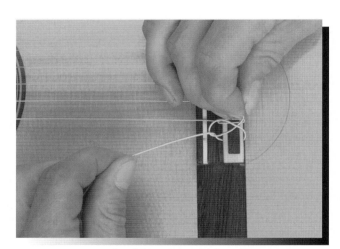

... wind it around itself ...

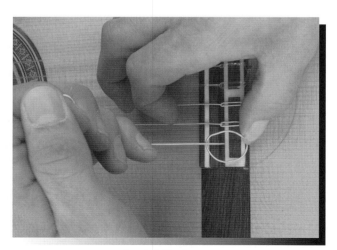

... hold it down ...

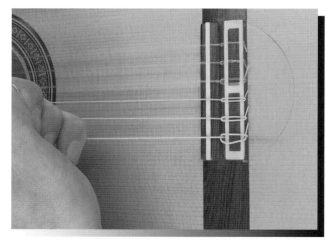

... and pull it tight.

This is what you do at the guitar head:

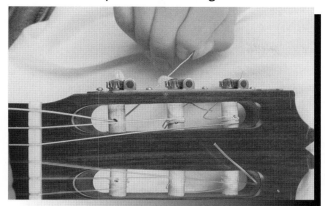

Insert the string ...

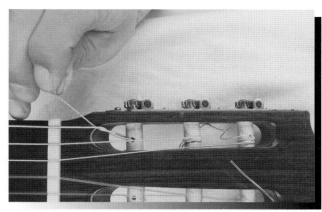

... wind it around itself ...

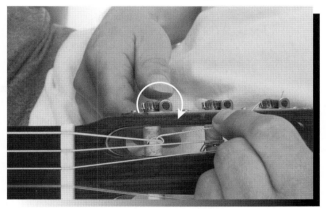

... and pull it tight.

It is much easier to change strings on a steel-string acoustic or electric guitar because you don't need to wind the string around itself.

In Good Shape – The Fingernails

As mentioned before, the left-hand fingernails must be trimmed short (see page 21).

The right-hand fingernails can be short as well. However, your playing will sound more beautiful and clear if you let them grow two to four millimeters above the fingertip. Shape them in the form of your fingertip by means of a nailfile because this shape is the best for plucking the strings. Any rough edges or corners create an unpleasant tone and wear out the strings as well. If you want a really comfortable feeling while playing, buy an especially smooth nailfile with which you can "polish" the front edge of the nails.

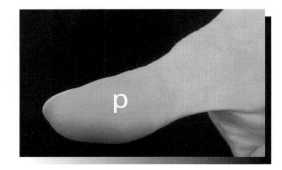

THE CD TRACKS – AND HOW TO USE THEM

Here is a listing of the CD contents. CDs are recorded in stereo; that means the CD-player has a different output on the two speakers. **L** refers to the left speaker and **R** to the right one. In the regular mix/set-up, student and teacher/accompaniment can be heard together. **Turn the balance knob of your CD-player all the way to the left; you will only hear your student's part. Turn it all the way to the right and you will hear the teacher's part or the other instruments.**
(The tuning tones are on both speakers.)

C Chords, Melodies And Much More ...

Acoustic guitars: Uli Türk and Helmut Zehe
Electric guitars and voice: Uli Türk
Keyboards and MIDI-arrangement: Uli Türk
Recorded by Uli Türk at Tonkopf-Studio, Reichshof
Produced bt Helmut Zehe and Uli Türk for Voggenreiter

WHAT'S WHERE? GLOSSARY

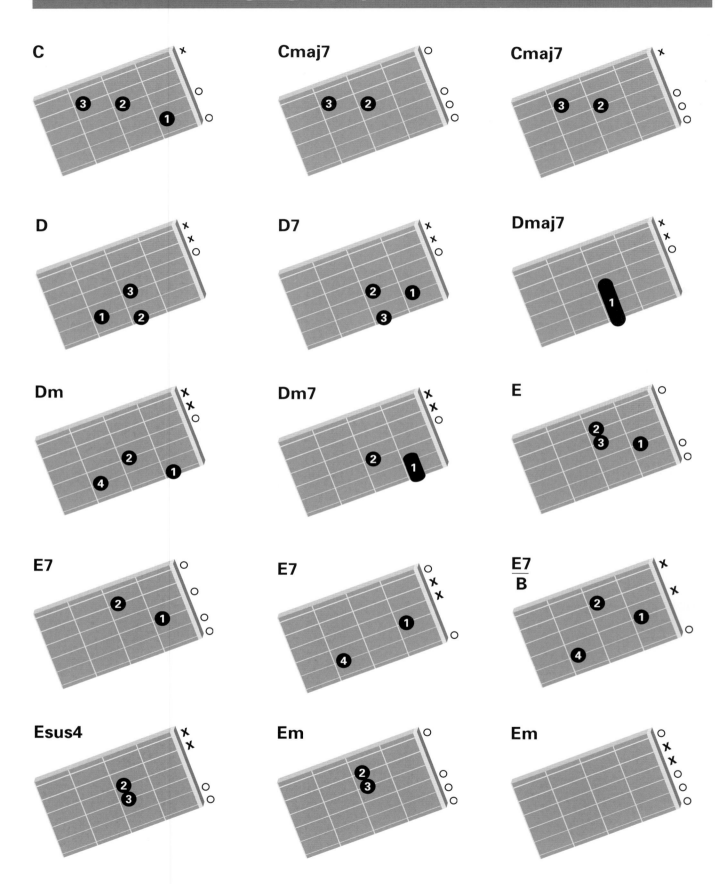

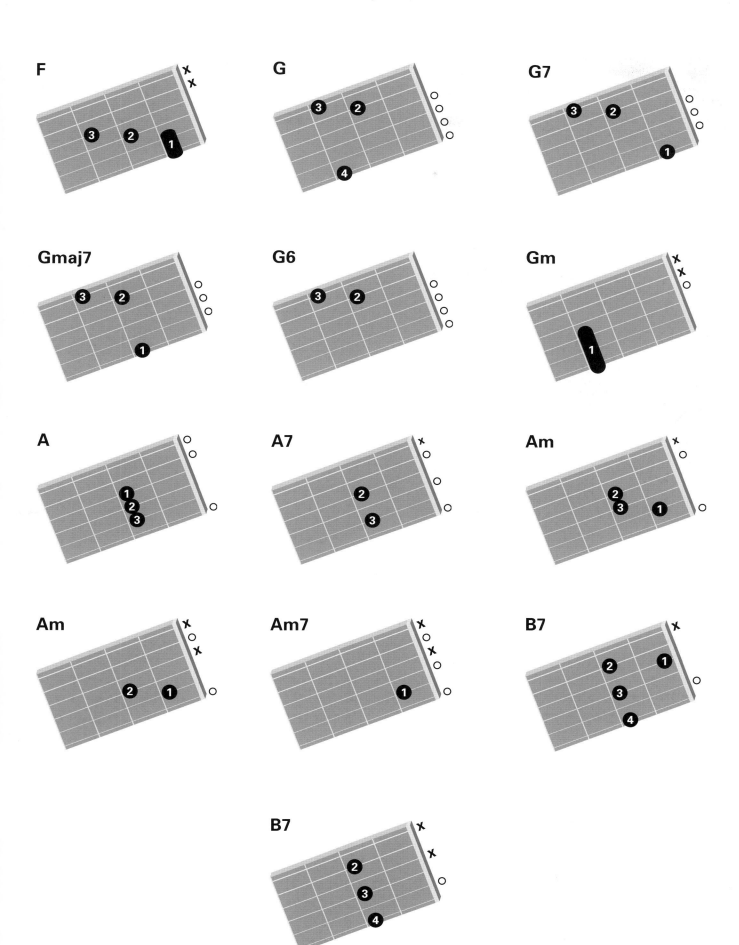

Helmut Zehe

Uli Türk

Since he was four, music has been the center of Helmut Zehe's life. At the age of five, he convinced his mother to ask every music teacher in town to teach him an instrument, no matter which. It cost him a lot of patience to wait until he turned seven and was finally accepted to attend the elementary class of the local music school. That's when he picked up the guitar. For several years, Helmut also played the violin and was a member of the school orchestra. At the age of seventeen, he was the singer and guitarist of a rock band, played in a guitar and mandolin orchestra and had his own students.

After Helmut finished school, he moved to Cologne and studied guitar at the Staatliche Musikhochschule. During that time he played in different ensembles and performed numerous concerts of classical

Uli Türk was born in 1955 in Neuwied, Germany.

In 1972 he started studying classical guitar at the Musikhochschule in Cologne and worked as a guitar teacher at different music schools until 1975. Since 1998, he has worked as a guitar teacher at Musikschule Rösrath/Overrath.

From 1979 until 1988, Uli accompanied Lutz Görner, an acknowledged recitor of German literature. During these ten years, he played about 2,000 shows, made 20 records (*such as Brecht/Texte and Lieder zur Lage der Nation, Die Bibel, Goethe für Alle, Fahrlässig umgebracht, Balladen für Kinder, Goethe für Kinder, Wilhelm Busch/Max und Moritz, Die fromme Helene*) and performed numerous times on TV and on the radio.

and contemporary chamber music. He often worked in the studio recording for TV and radio and making records. He rarely performed solo but focused on the music that enabled him to play in various groups.

Helmut enjoys introducing other people to music and especially to his beloved guitar. He loves teaching and is always trying to discover new alleys. He studied with various acknowledged guitarists and was a teacher at the University Cologne, Musik-hochschule Cologne and Rheinische Musikschule.

For many years now, Helmut has been working both as a guitar teacher and a performing artist. More than 70 of his compositions, instructional books and publications have been published by ORFEO21 in Cologne. Helmut is the director of the Städtische Musikschule Rösrath/Overath near Cologne.

In 1986, he single-handedly produced his first recording for children, which was followed by various productions for children (*1990: LiLalutsche* with Katja Ebstein). In 1990, he started the series "Gedichtezeit", which presents famous *German poetry* (*Goethe, Heine, Kästner, Morgenstern*).

Since 1990, Uli has been a freelancer for state radio WDR. He has worked on numerous radio plays, radio features and reports. In 1995, he wrote and hosted 24 sequels of the radio show *Music memory* for WDR3. In 1990 and 1991 he made two films for children about the German poets Heinrich Heine and Christian Morgenstern. He has written music for TV movies (e.g. *Eine Liebe in Istanbul*, ZDF) and has composed songs for the popular children TV show *Sendung mit der Maus* since 1988.

In 1990 he composed songs for Katja Ebsteins music program *Frauenlyrik*.

Uli's publications *Das romantische Gitarrenbuch 2* and *Das klassische Gitarrenbuch für Fortgeschrittene* were published by Voggenreiter in 1995 and 1997.

After many years spent in his own recording studio, Uli returns to performing on stage in 1997. He creates the program *Heine für Kleine* with his daughter Julia; their tour takes them through 50 German cities. Two years later, he goes back on the road with the sequential program *Goethe & Co.*, another stage production for children.

Uli Türk is married and lives with his wife Petra and his children Julia, Tim and Miriam in an old house in the Bergisches Land.

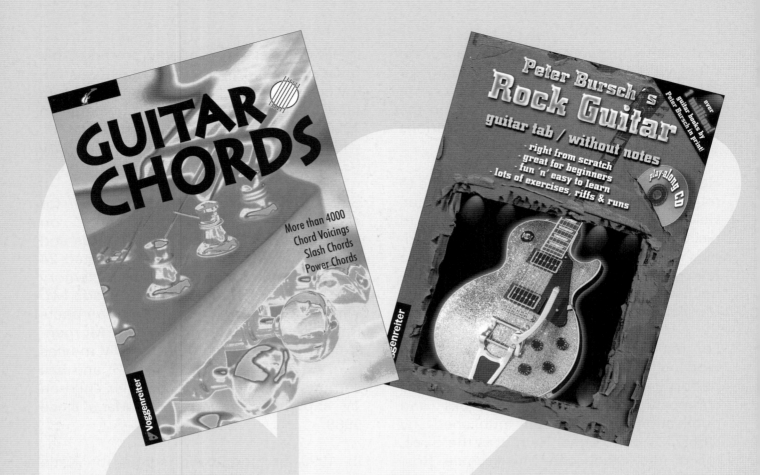

Voggenreiter

www.voggenreiter.de